Your

LOVE LIFE

REV. DR. CHESTER R. COOK

True Love Stories from an Airport Chaplain

Printing: PrintSource, Newnan, GA. www.printsource.net

CONTENTS

INTRODUCTION

Are you happy with your love life?

As I began to search the libraries for a book on the subject of love I was disappointed by what I found. I found a lot of books with love in the title but very few that really addressed the subject and substance of love. Many authors marketed sensual love as a bait to lure the prospective buyer to select their book. Other authors addressed a convoluted idea of love to give the reader some sense of personal accomplishment. But when I opened the covers, the books betrayed their titles.

A similar parallel exists in the world. There is a lot of talk about love and a great deal of sensual love but very little substantive love. In truth what is passed off as love in our relationships and in our churches is an artificial substitute.

Love is a word in the English language that is used in many contexts with a variety of meanings and nuances. A few of the many contexts of love include poetry, music, movies and television. Through these sensory mediums the common meaning for the word "love" has devolved into a sensual definition of feeling and self-gratification. This base definition of love pervades our contemporary society. This sensual meaning of love is also pervasive in our religious communities. When I read the Biblical accounts of love and looked at the love Jesus practiced, I became disenchanted with what was being taught and what I was experiencing in real life. I also became dissatisfied with my level of comprehension and competence in the area of love.

So began my quest for love. I determined to find out everything I could about love. I determined to become love and practice perfect love.

I am not claiming to have apprehended love, only that it is the supreme goal. Without the supreme goal, to become love and the discipline to practice perfect love, I would still be struggling in my ignorance and wandering in discontentment.

At this point your human nature may be resistant to reading on. You may feel hesitant to read on. You may be saying to yourself I don't want to read on. This is because our carnal nature will resist surrendering to the way of love. Without love our lives will be fruitless, purposeless and meaningless. It is imperative that you read on for your sake and for the sake of the gospel.

I believe the reason why the Church and Christians have not transformed the world as Jesus Christ ordered, is because we have failed to "be love".

God loves you, Jesus loves you, and I love you so much that we offer you this invitation to participate in, and become, this perfect love.

Make a Wish

I received a call from the Delta Care Team requesting my assistance at Gate B12. The Delta Care Team is a specially trained association of Delta employees that provide critical incident assistance in emergency situations.

I proceeded to the gate where I was met by a Delta employee. The employee explained to me that the aircraft pulling into the gate was inbound from Orlando, Florida and that there was a death on board the aircraft. Seconds later the fire department paramedics arrived along with Chaplain Thomas Houston, the chaplain of the Atlanta Fire Department Airport Division. We entered the aircraft while the passengers were disembarking. The faces of the passengers were full of tears and shock.

As we arrived in the First Class cabin we were greeted by the pilot and a lead flight attendant. I could see past them into the center isle a pale young boy being embraced by his father. The boy was wearing a tee-shirt with Mickey Mouse on the front.

Flight attendants standing in the row on either side of the father and son were trying to block the view while directing the passengers off the craft.

Passengers filing out on the left and right were rubbernecking and gasping as they walked by the flight attendants.

The flight attendants, while doing an exemplary job, were also caught in the emotion of the moment as they were fighting back tears.

Every passenger that filed by became another challenge not to break down into a full blown cry. A couple of flight attendants unable to process the emotion were in the galley crying.

The pilot was a little strained for words but managed to explain the situation with grace. He explained that the boy was a victim of cancer and that he had had a final wish to go to Walt Disney World in Orlando. The flight and vacation was a Make A Wish grant to the boy and his family.

I carved my way past the exiting passengers to sit next to the father holding his beloved son. I placed my hand on his back to provide some comfort. The Father was wearing an airbrushed shirt with a Bible verse on the front which said, "I Can Do All Things Through Christ Who Strengthens Me." Philippians 4:13 and on the back which said, "No, In All Things We Are More Than Conquerors, Through Him who Loved us," Romans 8:37. It turns out that he was a Christian preacher in a small church in North Georgia.

As I began to minister to him, he ministered to me. He told me that his son Timmy was a Christian and that he had leukemia, but his final wish on earth was to go to Walt Disney World, in Orlando. He continued saying that Timmy had the best three days of his life in Walt Disney World in Orlando, but just before he died told me he had one final wish, to be in Heaven with Jesus.

He said to me that he and the boy's mother had been preparing for this moment and said "This is not a time for crying but a time for celebration because Timmy got his final wish."

As I looked around the cabin the mood was still very sad. The lead attendant came to me and said that several of the crew and remaining passengers wanted to know if we could say a prayer. So Chaplain Houston and I gathered the grieving attendants and passengers in a circle around Timmy and the father.

As I prayed the crew and passengers openly expressed their grief.

I prayed,

"Loving God and Christ, Timmy is in your loving arms in Heaven. He is a beautiful boy and he is loved. Thank you for the wonderful years you gave to Timmy, with his mother and father. Comfort all who grieve and help us to celebrate with the family, that hope of eternal life with you. Thank you for making his final wish come true. Amen."

As you continue to read you will be introduced to LOVE. This first story opens the reality of love in our lives. Chapter One will begin to open the teaching of love.

CHAPTER ONE

If you knew that you only had a few hours left to live,
What would your final words be?

Love, Love, Love

Love is probably the most important word in all the world. Love is also the most misunderstood word in the human vocabulary.

"Love, as I have loved…"

Jesus Christ made this statement, to his followers, just before his arrest and crucifixion.

This is the only "command" Jesus ever spoke, "LOVE." Those who would follow after Jesus have only one command to follow; love, love, love, seems simple enough.

In the Gospel of John 15:9, Jesus tells his followers,

"As God has loved me, so have I loved you."

Jesus does not begin with himself; he begins with God and says to his disciples, **"As God has loved me."** Jesus begins with the love that God had lavishly bestowed upon him. The love Jesus experienced was a divine love from the very Being of Love. God is the origin of love. In this discourse, Jesus is referring to God's divine love. Jesus wants his followers to clearly understand the source and proper definition of love; therefore, he qualifies the proper definition of love by explicitly connecting the meaning of love, to the love he has received from God. The love that Jesus experienced was not a love of this world. It was a divine love from heaven. This divine love from heaven is the essence of all true earthly love.

Jesus continues speaking and further connects the love he has received from God, with the love he is giving to his followers. Jesus says, **"so have I loved you."** Jesus having received God's love, in turn, loves the disciples in the same way God has loved him. Jesus makes this bold claim that his love for the disciples is equal to God's love for him.

"remain in my love"

Continuing on in John 15:9, Jesus exhorts his followers to remain "in" his love. Ultimately, this is the point that Jesus is trying to convey. Jesus wants his followers to be "in" his love. Jesus is emphatic that his followers are to remain "in" his love and by remaining "in" his love they are by necessity remaining "in" God's love.

We have all experienced times in our lives when we are drawn off course and led to believe that happiness can be found in worldly pursuits. But when the pleasures of this world cease to satisfy, we are left feeling empty and dissatisfied. Jesus understands how easy it is to be distracted by worldly temptations. Jesus knows that the only way to find true happiness in this life is to stay connected to God through the love that Christ offers and to stay connected with each other through this same love. If we remain in love, God will use us. If we remain disconnected from love our life will become empty and our efforts in vain.

Coming home from work I have often received a welcome home hug from one of my boys, "I love you Dad," they would say. There is no greater joy in life than love being born and produced in the lives of the beloved. In the same way God desires love to be reproduced in the life of his children.

"If you obey my commands, you will remain in my love just as I have obeyed my Father's commands and remain in his love."

Jesus placed these words in the context of obedience. Obedience to Jesus is obedience to love. To obey love is to be love. Jesus could not have been more demanding of his followers. Jesus did not want there to be any confusion. If anyone claimed to be a disciple of Jesus then they needed to be the embodiment of his love. Jesus required his followers to be **disciples of love**. On this matter there was no compromise. A disciple of Jesus was a disciple of love. Disciples of Jesus could be recognized by their love. Jesus shares this insight about how Christians should be perceived in the world in John 13:35 by saying, "They will know you are my disciple by your love."

"A new command I give you: Love one another.
As I have loved you, so you must love one another.
By this all men will know that you are my disciples,
if you love one another." – John 13:34-35

As a father I have offered love to my children and the boundless provision of all that is good. But as a father I have forbidden that which is unloving, activities that lead to sin, death and destruction. All that is of love I give to you but that which is not of love will lead to your demise. In the same way God offers "all the trees of the garden," except, "the tree of the knowledge of good and evil, for when you eat thereof you will surely die." It is a matter of love and trust. Do you trust God? Do you trust love? Love always trusts.

Image of the Grape Vine

"I am the vine, you are the branches" – John 15:5

Jesus provides the image of being a conveyor of love, a vine; receiving the life giving nurture of God's love, and allowing the Love of God to flow through the vine into the life of the branches, where it will bear fruit. The love that originates from God flows through the vine (Jesus), into the branches (Believer), and ultimately into the fruit where it is manifested as the fruit of love. Believers become conduits of love and the fruit of love to the world. Jesus asked, "Can a good tree bear both good and bad fruit?" Can a vine filled with love bare anything but love?

"...and, my Father is the gardener. He cuts off every branch in me that bears no fruit." – John 15:2

The gardener prunes off every branch that is barren. Branches without love flowing through their veins are cut off, leaving only mature healthy branches full of love and fruit. The branch must remain in the vine to produce fruit. Remain in the vine and remain in love and you *will* produce the luscious fruit of love. "The fruit of the Spirit is love..." Galatians 5:22

Jesus provides no options to his followers but to love, not as the world loves but as God loves and as Christ loves. As one encounters a follower of Jesus Christ, love should be the overwhelming experience. The Spirit of Love flowing through the believer is mysteriously realized by the encountered, as the Love of God flowing through us.

"But this was not all He showed me, nor one half. As I thought of the Vine and the branches, what light the blessed Spirit poured direct into my soul! How great seemed my mistake in having wished to get the sap, the fulness out of Him. I saw not only that Jesus would never leave me, but that I was a member of His body, of His flesh and of His bones. The vine now I see, is not the root merely, but all-root, stem, branches, twigs, leaves, flowers, fruit: and Jesus is not only that: He is soil and sunshine, air and showers, and ten thousand times more than we have ever dreamed, wished for, or needed. Oh, the joy of seeing this truth! I do pray that the eyes of your understanding may be enlightened, that you may know and enjoy the riches freely given us in Christ." – Hudson Taylor

A "New Commandment"

"My command is this: Love each other as I have loved you."
– John 15:12

I cannot over emphasize the importance of this scripture. The setting for this command is the Upper Room. Jesus knows that in a few hours he will make the final sacrifice of love; he will give his life in obedience to the Will of God, at the cross. This final word to his family and closest friends is the heart of his teaching and life.

If you knew that you only had a few hours left to live, would you waste time talking about unimportant matters or fighting about meaningless differences? I doubt you would. My final words to my family and closest friends would be the same as Jesus': Love!!!

This "new" commandment is the only command for those who would follow after Jesus Christ.

How is Love Possible?

Love like God. This is the challenge of all who would follow after Jesus Christ. This is the command of Jesus Christ to anyone that would dare to claim Christ as his or her Master. Christians claim to believe in Jesus. But, can one believe in Jesus, in name only? Can one believe in Jesus and not believe in his message? To believe in Jesus Christ is to believe in Jesus as God's Son and to believe in Jesus Christ is to believe in what Jesus believed in.

Many have attempted to portray a Jesus other than the Jesus of the Bible. If the message of Jesus is altered to conform to some humanly conceived philosophy then I would argue that it is not the real Jesus but a false counterfeit Jesus. A non-loving Jesus is a fake; a Jesus made in our agenda; a Jesus made to fit our worldly desires. The way of the Biblical Jesus was the way of love.

"To believe in Jesus is to believe in what Jesus believed in. Jesus believed in love."
– Chester Cook

It is not possible to believe in Jesus and not believe in what he taught. Jesus and his word are inseparable. The Jesus of the Bible was the moral exemplar of love. He believed in love, he taught love and he practiced love.

Jesus believed in love. Jesus equated love with obedience to his words. Why? Because, Jesus loved with every ounce of his being and required the same of his followers. The words of Jesus were admonitions to love; not out of a legalistic duty but out of a desire to know and experience the power of God's love flowing through our being.

"But if anyone obeys his word, God's love is truly made complete in him. This is how we know we are in him:" – 1 John 2:5

Consider the instruction that a mother gives to her child, "Don't play with electricity." it is a command but in a more primary sense it is a loving admonition to keep the child from harm. In the same way love and obedience to love are one in the same. Legalistic submission to a list of commandments is not what is desired; rather, the higher aspiration is to see the child function in love by trusting the word of the mother; thereby, fulfilling the original intent of the mother's love to keep the child safe from harm. If the child fails to trust the mother's word then two choices follow; the child will obey out of fear of the mother's punishment or the child will disobey and suffer the consequences of their disobedience.

"We love because He first loved us." – 1 John 4:19

Divine Love is possible because God first loved us. We are able to love as God loves when we allow God to love through us. Divine love on earth is manifest when we commit ourselves to trust God, receive the true Jesus, follow his way of love, and please God.

Jesus defines love

Speaking in Aramaic, a Jewish language of the first century, the term "rakhma", would have been spoken, which means unconditional love. In the Greek text, the word for unconditional love was translated "agape." We have no word for such an attitude in English. This is why the western church has such a difficulty teaching love "agape," with success. The love taught in most churches is usually a selfish love known as "eros" or a friendship love known as "phileo". In some cases Christians reference family love "storge". This term has some common elements but still fails to encompass the total depth of "agape."

Agape

Agape is a Greek word that is commonly used to describe, unconditional love; God's Divine Love.

Agape is not based on emotions.

Agape is not egalitarian.

Agape is not reciprocal.

Agape is a covenant.

Agape is unilateral.

Agape is altruistic.

Agape, is a commitment of the will; a covenant made with God and self. I will be a person of perfect love.

Agape is the willful giving of oneself for the wellbeing of another.

Storge

Storge is a Greek word that is commonly used to describe family love or a love that grows out of friendship.

Phileo

Phileo is a Greek word that is commonly used to imply friend or friendship love.

Eros

Eros is a Greek word derived from the name of the Greek god Eros; generally refers to sensual love.

STORY TWO

Sojourner

Occasionally someone will walk into the Airport Chapel that I refer to as a sojourner. A sojourner is a person that is journeying from place to place based on a feeling or "spiritual unction."

Last year, over one of the bowl weekends, such a person wandered into the Airport Chapel, his name was Vinson. Vinson came to Atlanta to witness to the fans of a bowl game. He was young and carefree and a very likeable guy.

In the chapel I was trying to help a young "missionary" couple get to New Orleans but the fares were very expensive and the bus was not scheduled for New Orleans.

Out of the blue Vinson said he felt compelled of the Lord to give the couple a ride to New Orleans. After talking with Vinson for a few minutes they felt assured that Vinson was a good person and agreed to take him up on his offer. As they walked away I wondered, was this a divine appointment?

On the Monday following the bowl weekend I arrived at work and found a raw looking fellow standing in front of the Chapel door. He had spiked hair and several metal objects hanging from his ears and protruding out of his lips and eyebrows. His face was covered with gothic tattoos.

He asked me if I was the Chaplain? To which I responded, "Yes how may I help you?"

He told me his name was Dagon and that he was a Wiccan. He began to tell me how he and his girl (who was elsewhere in the airport) had been waiting since Sunday night in the Airport because the transmission and engine in their car had blown up just out of Atlanta. He said they needed to get home to Augusta but did not have money.

After talking with him for a few minutes he told me that Wiccans believed in self and in the natural powers. I asked him if he believed in God and he said that god was an invention of man. He said that men use the idea of god to put fear into people and to control people.

I replied that I didn't fear God but that I loved God and found God to be loving and kind. I challenged him to be open to God. I told him that God would prove Himself to him through His goodness.

I told Dagon to find his girlfriend and I would see if I could find any help for them. I turned my efforts to trying to find some way to get them to Augusta. Again the airfares and bus were not very encouraging. I was disappointed that I was not able to provide good news.

I returned to the chapel and found that Vinson had returned from New Orleans. He was talking to Dagon. Dagon was on the ropes. I overheard Vinson say, "You can have my car."

I was shocked.

Vinson turned to me and said, "My Uncle paid for my tickets to Paris, France and I am leaving tonight. I was going to ask you if you knew anyone that needed a car? But God provided me an answer already. The Lord told me to give my car to Dagon."

Dagon was very spiritually convicted by Vinson's generous gift. He thanked Vinson. Vinson handed Dagon the keys and title but said someone will have to pay the airport parking and fill the tank. I agreed to do both.

Vinson took his Bible and read this verse to Dagon, "Don't you know that the reason God is good to you is because he wants you to turn to him?" Romans 2:4

Vinson left to catch his flight and I took Dagon and his girlfriend to get the car out of parking and to get a tank of gas. They dropped me off back at the airport and said, "You know, God is good." I prayed for them and bid them a safe journey home.

I received an e-mail from Vinson several days later that read, "I really felt the Holy Spirit moving when I was in the Chapel at the Airport. God is Good."

CHAPTER TWO

Love the Lord

L-O-V-E is a simple acronym that will help us to learn to love as Christ loves.

L the first letter of the acronym stands for,
Love the Lord your God.

The Shema, Deuteronomy 6:5-7, is a prayer or confession that Jesus learned from his childhood. This prayer would have been a central part of his normal daily routine. The confession prayer would have been a part of his morning prayers, a hermeneutic for interpreting scripture, and a key to understanding his relationship with God.

"Love the Lord your God with all your heart, with all your soul,
and with all your strength... Impress them on your children. Talk
about them when you sit at home and when you walk along the
road, when you lie down and when you get up."
– Deuteronomy 6:5-7

A love relationship with the Lord God is our starting place. When we get the first button right all of the other buttons begin to line up as well.

When we are in love with someone we want to be with them, we want to know more about them, we want to feel their presence, we want to behold them. Our love for God becomes our passion. Our heart longs for our beloved. The mind, the will, and our emotions all reach out for our beloved. And with all our strength we pursue our beloved.

Loving with all our heart identifies the center of our being. With every beat of our heart we exist in God. The soul identifies our emotional being. Through our soul we express our deepest intimacy towards God. Love's power draws our physical body into worship and service.

> *"Jesus said unto him, You shall love the Lord your God*
> *with all your heart, and with all your soul,*
> *and with all your mind.*
> *And the second is like unto it,*
> *You shall love your neighbor as yourself."*
> – Matthew 22:37-39

Jesus is speaking to a Jewish lawyer, who asks him, "Teacher, which is the greatest commandment in the law?" Jesus quotes Deuteronomy 6:5 (the Shema), and includes the word "mind" in the equation. By including our mind Jesus completes the wholeness of being. He knows that the mind is the intelligence center of the human self. In the mind the will of man and the ability to covenant is realized. The ability to make a willful covenant with God is primary to the proper exercise of agape love. Remember agape love is a commitment of the will for the wellbeing of another.

Jesus continues and reminds the Jewish leaders of a text in Exodus which completes the definition of love to include neighbors. For Jesus the amendment to the Shema to love others is essential.

The lawyer wisely replies "You are right, Teacher... love is much more that all the burnt offerings and sacrifices." To which Jesus replies, "You are not far from the Kingdom of God." Mark 12:32.

Universal Love

"I have made a covenant of love for a thousand generations."
— Deuteronomy 7:7

The Hebrew people were blessed with a covenantal love. God promised to love the Hebrew people unconditionally. "Hesed" is a Hebrew word that is defined as willful, unconditional love. God loved the Hebrew people, not because they were deserving or special; God loved them by His choice. Those who loved God in return, God further promised to be their God.

"What does the LORD require of you but to do justice, steadfast love, and to walk humbly with your God?"
— Micah 6:8

God wanted the Hebrew people to be a witness to the world; not just to the Hebrews, but somewhere along the way the Hebrew people began to convey God as proprietary. In a sense the Hebrew people brought God down to the level of a tribal deity. The love that God expressed for all of his creation was horded by the select few. This was not God's intention. God desired his love to be universal to all mankind.

Jesus attempted to restore the Hebrew people to their fundamental teachings, to be one with God in love and to be a witness to the world that God is love. Jesus also exemplified this divine love to the people he encountered.

The Lord of Love

Several scripture texts refer to God using the metaphor of Lover. God is described as the loving father, loving husband, or loving groom. Conversely, the Jewish people and the church are referred to as the beloved. While all metaphors are limited, the image of God is consistent. God is always conveyed as the eternal source of love. We on the other hand, the beloved, are often portrayed as unfaithful, uncommitted and unloving. The beloved's preoccupation is her own pursuit of selfish wants and desires, worldly pleasures, and temporal lust. It is therefore important to visualize God as the Lord of Love; in other terms, the one who is "The Master of Love."

"Life minus love equals zero."
– Rick Warren

Remember how Romeo and Juliet abandoned everything for love. Now stop and consider how we would feel about Juliet, had Romeo shown up that night on the balcony only to find Juliet with another man? The story would have had a different ending. Our love for God has to be our sole passion. Love for God must be our heart's desire. We must guard our hearts from allowing any other desire from diminishing our love for God.

Hosea and Gomer

The story of Hosea and Gomer is offered as a hyperbole of God's love for the beloved. Hosea's love for his wife Gomer is unexplainable. He demonstrates a devotion and passion towards Gomer that is divinely inspired.

"When the LORD began to speak through Hosea, the LORD said to him, "Go, take to yourself an adulterous wife and children of unfaithfulness, because the land is guilty of the vilest adultery in departing from the LORD. So he married Gomer...The LORD said to me, "Go, show your love to your wife again, though she is loved by another and is an adulteress. Love her as the LORD loves the Israelites, though they turn to other gods and love the sacred raisin cakes." – Hosea 1:3; 3:2

Hosea is instructed by God to love Gomer. Hosea has a love for Gomer that defies emotion, reason, and logic. Hosea's love epitomizes the Love of God for Israel. Hosea's love for Gomer is covenantal. No activity, indiscretion or impropriety on the part of Gomer has any affect on the permanence of Hosea's love. Gomer on the other hand is portrayed as the epitome of unrequited love. Gomer continues in her adulteress ways and Hosea redeems her out of a life of prostitution.

After a life of unfaithfulness and adulterous living Hosea is instructed to buy back his wayward wife and show her love. The love Hosea demonstrates for Gomer is paramount to the love God has for Israel. It is also a metaphor for the redemption of the bride of Christ; as Hosea pays her a bride-price.

Paternal Love

When a child is conceived there is a maternal and paternal love for the child even before it is born. After birth, love for the child continues to grow and mature. The bond of love in families is a foretaste of God the Father and His love for His children.

Jesus conveyed his relationship to God as one of a son to a father. God is "Abba," (Father); a Dad who loves the Son. This image of God as Father, while resident in the scriptures, was troublesome to the people of Jesus' day. Jesus used the familial name, Father, in all of his prayers except one. Jesus even taught his followers to pray to and address God as our Father who is in Heaven.

The metaphor of God as a loving father is presented in the story of the prodigal son. The Father maintains an unconditional familial love for the wayward son.

"When he came to his senses, he said, 'How many of my father's hired men have food to spare, and here I am starving to death! I will set out and go back to my father and say to him: Father, I have sinned against heaven and against you. I am no longer worthy to be called your son; make me like one of your hired men.' So he got up and went to his father. But while he was still a long way off, his father saw him and was filled with compassion for him; he ran to his son, threw his arms around him and kissed him." – Luke 15:18-20

Here Comes the Bride

The metaphor of God as the Groom is replete in the scriptures. Many of the patriarchs and matriarchs are prototypes of our relationship with God. Jesus is the exemplar of the Groom and his beloved, the Bride.

Aluen, in his classic book "Christus Victor," considers theories of salvation and the conception of God. Aluen concludes, "Divine Love prevails over the Wrath, the Blessing overcomes the Curse, by the way of Divine self-oblation and sacrifice." (Aluen, p. 153)

God created the universe with love as his sole purpose. This Divine Love is in the universe moving towards the ultimate consummation of God's love. God created humanity with a free will so that individuals could respond of their own accord to love. If humanity had been created without a will to choose, love would not be possible. Love must be free to choose. Love cannot be demanded or coerced. Even though God loved his creation, His love could not force his beloved to respond. Such a response could only come from the beloved of free will. God's love called out to the beloved and continued to offer the beloved an invitation of love. God courts and romances and proposes and patiently waits for the reply of the beloved.

The community that God is establishing is made up of those who have accepted, submitted, yielded, surrendered, and received God's love. When we become intimate with God's Love we become vessels of love. We become one with God.

"For this reason a man will leave his father and mother and be united to his wife, and the two will become one flesh."
– Genesis 2:24

"This is a profound mystery–but I am talking about Christ and the church." – Eph 5:32

The passion of God to be one with the beloved is personified in the wedding banquet. Jesus experienced this consummation in its fullest and expressed his desire for all to enter into the Divine Feast.

"'Let us rejoice and be glad and give him glory! For the wedding of the Lamb has come, and his bride has made herself ready. Fine linen, bright and clean, was given her to wear.' Then the angel said to me, 'Write: 'Blessed are those who are invited to the wedding supper of the Lamb!'" – Revelations 19:7-9

Gene Roddenberry, the creative mind behind "Star Trek" is one of my favorite theologians. Even though he is a very unorthodox theologian, his episodes usually contained moral and theological connotation. In the first motion picture titled, "Star Trek the Movie," the plot involves the exploration of space by a communication satellite called "Voyager." The mission of

> *"O Lord, you have made us for thyself and our hearts are restless until they rest in thee."*
> – St. Augustine of Hippo

Voyager is to traverse the universe and gather all of the knowledge of the cosmos. After completing the assignment, Voyager returns to earth to finish the final download of the program and knowledge. However, the knowledge Voyager has gained presents a dilemma. Voyager now realizes that it has a creator and wants to be one with its creator. Voyager destroys the connection hardware which forces the creator to transmit the final code in person.

We all have a void in our heart that longs for love and this void can only be filled by the Creator of Love. Here the mystery of the universe has been revealed. "Christ in you, the hope of glory." Colossians 1:27.

"On that day you will realize that I am in my Father, and you are in me, and I am in you… Jesus answered and said unto him, If a man love me, he will keep my words: and my Father will love him, and we will come unto him, and make our abode with him."

– John 14:20-23

Christmas in July

One hot Wednesday morning in July, I was walking across the Atrium in the main Terminal, when an airport employee stopped me in the Atrium alerting me to a couple he had just directed to the Airport Chapel, Billy and Sally. This young married couple found themselves stranded, hungry and homeless in the Atlanta Airport. To make matters more complicated Sally was seven months pregnant.

Billy and Sally traveled to Atlanta in their small car, on the promise of a job offer but when they arrived the job had already been given to another individual. Billy and Sally used what money they had to stay in a local hotel but when their money ran out they started sleeping in their car at night and living in the airport during the day. Billy began looking for any job he could find. He found a part time job working at a local Wendy's but they would only give him a few hours a week. In their desperation Billy and Sally continued to come to the Atlanta Airport in the hopes of finding a better job with more hours for Billy and the possibility of a job for Sally.

Having heard their story, I made haste to find this modern day "Mary and Joseph" at the Airport Chapel.

When I met Billy and Sally I was surprised at how young they were. Standing before me was a strong, trim, and handsome young man. He was wearing a letterman's jacket from his football team where he was a star receiver. His boyish smile reminded me of Will Smith the movie star. She was wearing a black outfit that looked like a prom dress. She was soft, trim, and beautiful, with a sweet smile, holding his arm. Together they looked like a homecoming king and queen. They were the quintessential high school sweethearts.

I listened to the story of the anxious couple and offered some words of encouragement and hope. I encouraged the young couple to draw upon their faith in God and on their beliefs of trust and love. I gave them my standard "trust, love and glorify" spiel and prayed with them. I asked them to believe in God's promise and expect a miracle. I told them that when we walked out the door to be prepared, because God would answer their prayer.

After praying I went to talk to the manager at Paschal's in the Atrium. Charles said that Paschal's had a hiring freeze but that he needed someone right away. I went back to tell Billy & Sally the hopeful news. After telling them, I took Billy over to meet Charles and find out the name of the HR Recruiter. When I asked Charles his name he told me, "Why don't you ask him yourself? He is standing right behind you in line."Standing in line right behind us was Hugh, the HR Recruiter. He gave Billy his card and told him to be at his office at 10:00 a.m. tomorrow morning. After hearing his story Hugh also said he would find a position for Sally.

Billy and Sally overflowed with excitement but their miracle was only partially fulfilled. I found them beds in local shelters, but the shelter could only accommodate them if they slept in separate facilities. The thought of being separated distressed Sally, which concerned Billy. I contacted the Atlanta Police Department HOPE Team for a CIT officer, they dispatched Officer Cruz. He took the couple in his squad car to several shelters but none of them were suited for a young married couple. When they arrived back at the airport, word came from the Aero Clinic that one of their employees had an extra room in her home that she wanted to offer to the young couple. Tears of joy and soft praise enveloped the young couple as they hugged each other and kissed.

Billy was given a job as at Paschal's and Sally was given a job working as a hostess at Houlihan's. Billy was also offered a second job by The Atlanta Bread Company working the midnight shift.

CHAPTER THREE

The Object of Love is Others

O the second letter of the acronym stands for,
The Object of Love is Others.

"I give you a new commandment, that you love one another."
– John 13:34 (NRSV)

O stands for the object of love, others.

Without an object to love, love becomes objectless. It ceases to have purpose. It ceases to exist.

There are two dimensions to love. We have already discussed the vertical dimension, loving God. For many this is an easy proposition, after all God lovingly reciprocates. The second dimension of love is the horizontal dimension, loving others. This dimension people find far more difficult because the object does not necessarily love in return.

Over my many years of ministry I have come to appreciate the work of General William Booth. General Booth was the founder of the Salvation Army. He led in spreading the good news of God's Love over much of the world. He organized street meetings and evangelistic services where hundreds responded to invitation to be saved by faith in Jesus Christ. General Booth, in his senior years, became ill, his eyesight failed him, and one year he was in such bad health that he was unable to attend the Salvation Army Convention in London, England. General Booth sent a telegram message to be read at the opening of the convention.

As the thousands of delegates gathered at the convention, the moderator announced that General Booth would not be able to be present because of failing health and eyesight. Disappointment swept across the floor of the convention. A little light dispelled some of the darkness when the moderator announced that General Booth had sent a message to be read with the opening of the first session. He opened the message and began to read the following:

Dear Delegates of the
Salvation Army Convention:

Others! *Signed, General Booth*
"Others, Lord, Yes, OTHERS!
Let this my motto be,
Help me to live for OTHERS,
That I may live for Thee."

These words come from a poem of unknown authorship but whose origin must have been God. The entire poem reaffirms the object of love.

OTHERS!

"Lord help me to live from day to day,
In such a self forgetful way;
That even when I kneel to pray,
My prayer shall be for OTHERS.
Help me in all the work I do,
To ever be sincere and true;

> *And know that all I'd do for you,*
> *Must needs be done for OTHERS.*
> *Let "SELF" be crucified and slain,*
> *And buried deep; and all in vain,*
> *May efforts be to rise again,*
> *Unless to live for OTHERS.*
> *And when my work on earth is done,*
> *And my new work in heaven begun;*
> *May I forget the crown I've won,*
> *While thinking still of OTHERS.*
> *Others, Lord, Yes, OTHERS!*
> *Let this my motto be,*
> *Help me to live for OTHERS,*
> *That I may live for Thee."*

– Author Unknown

GOD EXTENDS AGAPE LOVE INCLUSIVELY!

True love is manifest in our agape love for others. Jesus Christ only knows one love and it is absolute. I have come to realize that most Christians fail to love as Jesus Christ loved because their agape love is reserved for family relationships or select individuals. This proprietary love is not the love Jesus envisioned for his followers. Jesus conceived of a love that was inclusive. The supreme love Jesus taught was not restricted to only the worthy. It was extended to all.

> *"Each one according to his means should take care to be at one with everyone else, for the more one is united to his neighbor, the more he is united with God."*
> – Dorotheos of Gaza

Everyone that Jesus encountered was offered this love. Many did not accept the love he offered but Jesus remained resolute.

Omni Love

Omni love is the essence of God's presence in the World. The omnipresent Love of God is extended to the World through the will and covenant of God.

God has willed to love us.

God loves us, period – end of discussion. God has further willed for us to love each other, period – end of discussion. There is no compromise on this point.

As disciples of love we are to love God and Christ and others. Omni love is inclusive of all who will receive. Anyone who practices exclusivity is acting contrary to the nature of love and will of God. Anyone who excludes themselves chooses willfully to remain outside of the community of love

This comprehensive love is the innate response of a Father to his children. God envisions all humankind as his children. God is the Father of all humankind. All human life is conceived in the image of God. As children in a family, our love, towards each other, is inherent.

Love for Enemies

"You have heard that the Law of Moses says, 'Love your neighbor and hate your enemy.' But I say, love your enemies! Pray for those who persecute you! In that way, you will be acting as true children of your Father in heaven. For he gives his sunlight to both the evil and the good, and he sends rain on the just and on the unjust, too. If you love only those who love you, what good is that? Even corrupt tax collectors do that much. If

you show love to your friends, how are you different from anyone else? Even pagans do that. But you are to be perfect, even as your Father in heaven is perfect." – Matthew 5:43-48

Some have found the joy of loving others, especially others who have shown an ability to love in return. Jesus spoke of the ease of loving others who love responsively. Jesus says that even tax collectors, publicans, and pagans, love their friends.

In the words of Jesus and the context of the Sermon on the Mount, God gives, "His sunlight to both the evil and the good … rain on the just and on the unjust." The point Jesus makes here is, **God's love is offered to both the good and evil and to the just and unjust**.

> *"The Bible tells us to love our neighbors, and also to love our enemies; probably because they are generally the same people."*
> – G. K. Chesterton

The love Jesus is referring to is more comprehensive than friendship (phileo) love. Jesus compares God's comprehensive love to the "sunlight" that falls on both good and evil men and to the "rain" that falls on the just and the unjust. God's love (agape) is omni present and not contingent on our worthiness or based on our goodness.

Jesus extends the reach of love to include even our enemies (brothers and sisters in rebellion). When we love our enemies Jesus says we are acting as "true children" of God. **In one way the inclusion to "love our enemies" makes love much easier to practice. Love is easier to practice because we no longer have to decide who may or may not be loved; the choice has already been made. We are to love all that God loves.**

> *"To love and be loved is to feel the sun from both sides."*
> – David Viscott

To be congruent with this teaching we as disciples should manifest this love to everyone; yes, even our enemies. The behavior of love we espouse should be the behavior we model. A world where everyone loves is what we propose to usher in. How can we expect others to love if we won't?

> *"Love is the difficult realization that something other than oneself is real."* – Iris Murdoch

Perfect Love

> *"All sorts of people are fond of repeating the Christian statement that 'God is Love'. But they seem not to notice that the words 'God is Love' has no real meaning unless God contains at least two Persons. If God was a single person, then before the world was made He was not Love. Of course, what these people really mean when they say 'God is Love' is often something quite different: they really mean Love is God."* – C. S. Lewis

The foundational principle of the Bible is,

God is Love

God loves the world

God loves us. God loves me. God loves you.

This good news (gospel) is the invitation that God offers, an invitation to respond to His love. When we respond to His invitation of love we become participants of God's perfect love.

> *"Be perfect, even as your Father in heaven is perfect."*
> – Matthew 5:43-48

If I can draw upon a supply of power from a Being greater than I, dwelling within me, then I can do perfectly what is humanly impossible – even service my enemy.

Consider God's perfect love to be the bull's eye in the center of a round target and the circles radiating outward to be the lessening degrees of love. As we move towards the center of the target the circles grow closer together until they become one with the center.

This is also true with regard to our love for others. The closer we get to God the more we love others and the more we love others the more we become like God's perfect love.

"No man has at any time [yet] seen God. But if we love one another, God abides (lives and remains) in us and His love (that love which is essentially His) is brought to completion (to its full maturity, runs its full course,) is perfected in us!"

– 1 John 4:12 (Amplified)

God's love and His invitation to participate in love has always been a constant. But, God's love and invitation to participate in love has been rejected by man. Our rejection of God and his love has brought about our own condemnation. Our unloving response to God and our unloving treatment of humanity is defined as Sin. The condition of Sin severed the lifeline of love with God from the human vantage point. By the activity of God through Jesus the love lifeline was repaired. God's invitation still exists but now it is mediated through Jesus Christ.

Jesus Christ is the mediator of this new invitation to be spiritually reconnected to God's love. Jesus made this spiritual fusion possible through his devotion to God and his consummation of humanity. In simple terms Jesus is holding the loving hand of the Father while reaching down to us with the other hand of love.

"It is impossible to love God without loving Jesus Christ."
– Chester Cook

Is it possible to love the Father and not love the Father's son? Could I say I love you but I do not love your child? To say one loves God without loving Jesus Christ is not reasonable. How can one love God and not love the perfect human example of love, Jesus Christ? How can someone reject perfect love? For a Muslim, a Buddhist, a Hindu or a Jew to say that I love God but I don't believe in Jesus, is incongruent, and an indication of religious indoctrination against Jesus or a religious prejudice against the name Jesus. To reject Jesus

Christ is to reject the perfect model of love. It is also a rejection of the only possibility of realizing God's new covenant of love.

"Jesus said, 'If God were your Father,
you would love me.'" – John 8:42

Hardened Hearts

There are some who are not responsive to love.

"But I know you, that ye have not the love of God in you."
– John 5:42

While it seems improbable, there are many people who are not receptive to an invitation of love. There are many spiritual, mental and environmental factors that bring someone to this state of denial where they have developed a hardened heart. There are many who will not love; someone else who will not love. This willful rejection to love creates a downward spiral of indifference and hate.

Jesus encountered people who rejected his love. We find it easy to point fingers at them. In truth many zealous Christians fall into this category. You may have encountered these unloving, judgmental people. They have a tendency to quote scripture and hurl judgment on individuals and groups; following policy while tearing people into pieces.

"The person who does not love himself is too empty of love to give it away… and feels too unworthy to accept it from God or from others." – Robert Schuler

The Good Samaritan

The story of the "Good Samaritan" is one of the greatest stories Jesus ever told.

In the story Jesus is confronted by a "lawyer" an expert in Jewish law. The purpose of the lawyer, as stated by Luke was, "he stood up to test Jesus." The lawyer asks, "Teacher, what must I do to inherit eternal life?"

Jesus in reply asks the lawyer to answer his own question.

The lawyer answers with the Shema, "Love the Lord," Deuteronomy 6:5 and "Love others" Leviticus 19:18.

"Love the Lord your God with all your heart and with all your soul and with all your strength and with all your mind; and, Love your neighbor as yourself."

Jesus replies, "You have answered correctly. Do this and you will live."

But the lawyer continues and tries to "justify" himself. The lawyer asks, "Who is my neighbor?"

Please read for yourself.

On one occasion an expert in the law stood up to test Jesus. "Teacher," he asked, "what must I do to inherit eternal life?" "What is written in the Law?" he replied. "How do you read it?" He answered: " 'Love the Lord your God with all your heart and with all your soul and with all your strength and with all your mind'; and, 'Love your neighbor as yourself.' " "You have answered correctly," Jesus replied. "Do this and you will live." But he wanted to justify himself, so he asked Jesus, "And who is my neighbor?" In reply Jesus said: "A man was going down from Jerusalem to Jericho, when he fell into the hands of robbers. They stripped him of his clothes, beat him and went away, leaving him half dead. A priest happened to be going down the same road, and when he saw the man, he passed by on the other side. So too, a Levite, when he came to the place and saw him, passed by on the other side. But a Samaritan, as he traveled, came where the man was; and when he saw him, he took pity

> *on him. He went to him and bandaged his wounds, pouring on oil and wine. Then he put the man on his own donkey, took him to an inn and took care of him. The next day he took out two silver coins and gave them to the innkeeper. 'Look after him,' he said, 'and when I return, I will reimburse you for any extra expense you may have.' "Which of these three do you think was a neighbor to the man who fell into the hands of robbers?" The expert in the law replied, "The one who had mercy on him." Jesus told him, "Go and do likewise."*
> – Luke 10:25-37

The religious people in this story were looked upon in this society as the ones who should have shown compassion to the man. But it was the Samaritan who demonstrated love. The Samaritans were a mixed race people who were despised by the Jews.

Jesus used this story as a means of defining "neighbor" and "love." Jesus is clearly saying - there is no justification or good reason for not showing love.

Being a disciple and obeying the Word of God, places the believer into a moral dilemma. Do we love the Bible more than we love God or God's children? The religious of Jesus' day were faced with a similar predicament. Did they love the Torah more than others? They were faced with the challenge of loving others over and against religious rules and pious polity. This predicament is described in the story of The Good Samaritan. Even though the Priest and the Levite were within their rights, it was the Samaritan who demonstrated God's love. It was the Samaritan who demonstrated love towards the man. The Samaritan represents a commoner or unreligious person. And yet even without the principles of piety the Samaritan acted in love.

In the Atlanta Airport thousands of travelers pass through the gates on a daily basis. At any given time of day you can walk the concourses and see people in distress and crisis. Most of the traveling passengers rush by not even noticing the people in need. Many times they may notice the distressed person but due to their flight schedule they hesitate to get involved and rush past to catch their flight.

The Bride that Would not be Denied

Eve, young and beautiful, full of energy, danced into the chapel, hair long and blond in waves like a curled ribbon cascading on her shoulders and down her back. She had a look in her eyes of love and hope, full of eagerness. She began to talk about her boyfriend, Adam, a Marine on active duty. As she spoke she seemed to disappear into a dream like trance as though her words were creating a virtual reality of him in the room. By her description of him he was strikingly handsome and Atlas strong. The most magnificent man in the world.

Eve told me that Adam was in Afghanistan on an extended tour of duty and that she communicated with him every day by Skype and e-mail. She said they were in love and that they wanted to get married but the war kept delaying their plans. She told me that Adam said the he would marry her "anywhere - anytime." She said that Adam was due to return in a few days for a two week R & R and then he would have to go back to Afghanistan for one more year.

Eve immediately got to the purpose of her visit, a surprise marriage. She wanted to surprise Adam with a surprise wedding at the airport when he got off the plane.

As you can probably guess I was a little wary but her formidable sales pitch persuaded me to listen on. She told me it would be a small service and that they would only need the Airport Chapel for a few minutes.

I said to her that since it involved a military soldier she would need to get a Military Chaplain to endorse the marriage and preform the surprise ceremony. If she could get a Military Chaplain to do the service I would make the chapel available. She left and in a few hours I received a phone call.

"Chaplain Cook this is Major Jones. I am a Chaplain in the Marine Corps and I have agreed to perform a service for Adam and Eve and I want to make sure that we can use the Airport Chapel?"

I replied, "If you are willing to do the service I will make the Airport Chapel available." Everything was set.

The day arrived and as I walked into the Atrium of the Atlanta Airport, I felt as though I was walking into a big Airport public relations event taking place. The Atrium had three television cameras from the local networks, a red carpet rolled out on the floor and red balloon arches at one end. I thought to myself this must be something big and important. As I walked toward the Airport Chapel out walks Chaplain Major Jones in full dress uniform with Eve dressed in her wedding gown or should I say costume. Eve was outfitted in a hot red corset with a ruffled train cascading to the floor. They were heading towards the arrival exit to meet Adam as he exited security.

The camera men all grabbed their cameras and in true paparazzi style they jockeyed for the best position as Adam rounded the corner in his green camouflaged fatigues. Eve rushed past the crowd toward her Marine as his eyes popped in approval and his arms opened wide to receive his bounding beauty. Eve jumped into his arms and they swung around in a joyful embrace. Following their pirouettes Eve looked into his eyes and said "you said you would marry me 'anywhere – any time.' Well this is 'anywhere' and this is 'anytime'."

Without hesitation Adam pulled Eve into his arms and kissed her.

Then he yelled, "WHOO WAH ! let's do it!"

The crowd all yelled, "WHOO WAH!"

They both walked to the red carpet and down the aisle to the red balloon archway where Chaplain Major Jones was waiting with his Bible to perform the traditional marriage ceremony.

CHAPTER FOUR

Love is a Vow

V the third letter of the acronym stands for,

Love is a Vow

The Hebrew word for covenant is "berit." The well known passage from Micah 6:8, illustrates God's covenant in human imagery.

"And what does the Lord require of you but to do justice and to love kindness and walk humbly with your God?" – Micah 6:8

The Hebrew term for "justice" is mishpat, the behavior required by the covenant. The Hebrew term for "to love kindness," is "hesed," it refers to the love that is expressed in a covenant, whereas another word, "ahabah," means love where no covenant is present.

Ahabah is an omnipresent, all-inclusive, pervasive love that covers all of God's creation. God's ahabah is a constant towards humankind.

Hesed is a contractual special love available to the beloved; a contract to convey by self obligation, action to, or the provision of fulfilling the promised term. It is unilateral in its conveyance but can be reciprocal in agreement. The desire of hesed is mutuality.

A covenant relationship comes about through interactions of entrusting and accepting entrustment. Entrusting is to be distinguished from trusting. To trust someone is to judge that the person is trustworthy. To entrust is not merely to trust in an inner sense of being disposed to the other but actually to place ourselves or something we value in the other's hands. To entrust is to take a risk that we might be betrayed. By entrusting we make ourselves vulnerable for the wellbeing of another. When we make a covenant to love we are entrusting ourselves knowing that we may be hurt; therefore, covenant love includes grace and forgiveness as a condition of compliance.

> *"Love God and do whatever you please: for the soul trained in love to God will do nothing to offend the One who is Beloved."*
> – St. Augustine of Hippo

I Will!

These two simple words "I will," will change our lives forever. The marriage covenant begins with this simple declaration of love. We fail to realize, that contained in this **vow** is a definition of a divine love that transcends time; agape (love).

Agape (love) is a commitment of the will for the well being of another.

Agape is a commitment of the will to love as God loves. Agape is, the unconditional giving of oneself for the well being of another; a covenant made between you and God to love someone. God is the only source for agape because God is the origin. Agape is not a love that comes from self; rather, agape is a conjoining of oneself with the Spirit, to allow the Spirit of Love to enter and become one with the beloved; thereby, channeling love to others as a flower offers its fragrance to the air.

Couples entering into marriage need to understand that the vow they are taking is a vow of agape; a personal inner commitment of their will to unconditionally devote their lives to their spouse. This devotion is not contingent on the worth or the reciprocation of the spouse; it is unilateral; a complete altruistic sacrifice of one life for another. The marriage vow anticipates the reciprocal covenant of the beloved but it is not coerced.

> *"To follow Jesus as an act of love means to trust him."*
> – Scot McKnight

When two people enter into marriage, a covenant is made, but few understand the depth of the vow they are making. Many enter into marriage believing that their physical attraction or feeling of love will sustain their marriage, but when the physical attraction wanes or the feelings of love falter the marriage begins to fail. Agape is more than a physical attraction or an emotional feeling. It is a sacrifice and surrender to the highest and noblest ambition of God, agape.

The covenant of marriage is expressed as a metaphor for Christ and his bride. The husband is counseled to love as Christ loves the church.

"Husbands, love your wives, just as Christ loved the church and gave himself up for her to make her holy, cleansing her by the washing with water through the word, and to present her to himself as a radiant church, without stain or wrinkle or any other blemish, but holy and blameless. In this same way, husbands ought to love their wives as their own bodies. He who loves his wife loves himself. After all, no one ever hated his own body, but he feeds and cares for it, just as Christ does the church – for we are members of his body. For this reason a man will leave his father and mother and be united to his wife, and the two will become one flesh. This is a profound mystery – but I am talking about Christ and the church." – Ephesians 5:25 NIV

The marriage of a groom and bride is a picture of the "profound mystery." The mystery revealed is the ultimate purpose of God in the consummation of creation. The union of a man and woman are symbolic of the uniting of the creation and the Divine made possible by the Christ event. Christ takes a bride in the church and the two mysteriously become one in the new creation. The consummation of the Divine and the human is realized by the indwelling Spirit of the Christ.

"Therefore shall a man leave his father and his mother,
and shall cleave unto his wife: and they shall be
one [Echad] flesh" – Genesis 2:24

"Echad" is "used to denote God." In Deuteronomy 6:4 and in many other passages "Echad" refers to a compound unity. When we compare "Echad" as used in other passages to Deuteronomy 6:4 we see that God is "not an Absolute One" but a "Compound Unity".

God's grace is present in that though nothing requires covenanting, God nevertheless sees fit to create a covenant, to our benefit. Even though God initiates each covenant, we must still decide whether we will accept it. Our freedom is not destroyed by God's initiative, and yet is severely constrained in that if we choose to refuse God's offer of a covenant, we reject an act of love.

Love is a Covenant

All covenants have conditions. Like legal contracts, covenants convey and establish terms and condition between the contracting parties. The covenant of love is predicated on the worth of the individual; not the merits of the individual. God values each person individually as a part of the community. God values each person uniquely, irreplaceably and equally.

"The time is coming," declares the Lord, "when I will make
a new covenant with the house of Israel and with the house
of Judah. It will not be like the covenant I made with their
forefathers when I took them by the hand to lead them out of
Egypt, because they broke my covenant, though I was a husband

to them," declares the Lord. "This is the covenant I will make with the house of Israel after that time," declares the Lord. "I will put my law in their minds and write it on their hearts. I will be their God, and they will be my people. No longer will a man teach his neighbor, or a man his brother, saying, 'Know the Lord,' because they will all know me, from the least of them to the greatest," declares the Lord. "For I will forgive their wickedness and will remember their sins no more."

– Jeremiah 31:31-34

General Covenant

General covenants are universal. They extend generalized coverage to the contracting parties. Like buying a car, bumper to bumper coverage is offered for a specified period of time. The love covenant is universal in that it conveys God's love to creation, without merit.

While it may be difficult to understand from a human viewpoint it is important to stress the value that love places on the individual and community. The proposal is of a supreme love that is egalitarian; that is to say a love that is offered at the highest degree to all. In practical terms, love for God, Jesus, father, mother, wife, husband, brother, sister, friend, stranger and enemy are all equal. This level of unconditional love is rejected by those who have rejected the love covenant and not easily comprehended by those inside the love covenant. But the fact remains; God is no respecter of persons.

"For whosoever shall do the will of God, the same is my brother, and my sister, and my mother."

– Mark 3:35

Special Covenants

Special covenants exist within the general covenant and provide contracting parties additional, extended, or amended conditions.

Special covenants offer privileges and obligations beyond the terms of the general covenant. Special covenants include marriage vows, children, employment, and legal contracts.

General covenants anticipate that the terms and conditions of special covenants will not violate or nullify the terms of the general covenant; rather the special covenants increase the responsibility to be compliant with both.

"The roses, the lovely notes, the dining and dancing are all welcome and splendid. But when the Godiva is gone, the gift of real love is having someone who'll go the distance with you. Someone who, when the wedding day limo breaks down, is willing to share a seat on the bus."
– Oprah Winfrey

When we vow to be married, we first honor our general covenant and secondarily vow with God and our betroved to be united in special covenant. When we covenant to have children we extend our responsibility to include God, wife and children. It is also true that as we enter into special utilitarian covenants, such as employment, mortgage or business, God requires full accountability to our subordinate vows or release from these covenants if they cannot be maintained.

"But the ministry Jesus has received is as superior to theirs as the covenant of which he is mediator is superior to the old one, and it is founded on better promises. For if there had been nothing wrong with that first covenant, no place would have been sought for another. But God found fault with the people and said: 'The time is coming, declares the Lord, when I will make a new covenant with the house of Israel and with the house of Judah. It will not be like the covenant I made with their forefathers when I took them by the hand to lead them out of Egypt, because they did not remain faithful to my covenant, and I turned away from them, declares the Lord. This is the covenant I will make with the house of Israel after that time, declares the

Lord. I will put my laws in their minds and write them on their hearts. I will be their God, and they will be my people. No longer will a man teach his neighbor, or a man his brother, saying, 'Know the Lord,' because they will all know me, from the least of them to the greatest. For I will forgive their wickedness and will remember their sins no more.' By calling this covenant "new," he has made the first one obsolete; and what is obsolete and aging will soon disappear."
– Hebrews 8:6-13

The general love covenant offered love to humanity, but when humanity rejected this relationship the consequence brought separation from God and death. God's love would not allow for the annihilation of humanity but God could and did by His own volition, provide a means of forgiveness and salvation, for those who would accept the invitation to be reconciled: Jesus Christ.

"For this reason Christ is the mediator of a new covenant, that those who are called may receive the promised eternal inheritance-now that he has died as a ransom to set them free from the sins committed under the first covenant."
– Hebrews 9:13

The general covenant of love is universal to all humanity and creation. The special covenant of Jesus Christ provides additional privileges, such as forgiveness, salvation, eternal life, promise, holiness, righteousness, and inheritance. Those outside the special covenant have no claim to its extended eternal benefits.

STORY FIVE

Home for the Holidays

Being at home has special meaning, especially over the holidays.

On Christmas Eve, I entered the Airport Chapel and caught a glimpse of what appeared to be a large man on the floor, balled up, face down in a fetal position. Occasionally, I observe people on the floor, someone praying or a homeless person trying to stealthily catch up on some sleep. But something was peculiar about this body.

As I approached, I could see his massive biceps ripping out of his red Affliction tee-shirt. Every inch of the skin on his arm was a canvas of tattoos. Across the back of his neck scrolled a large, red tattoo with the word "BLOODS" inked into his flesh.

I was frightened and cautious as I reached out my hand to touch the arch of his back. I felt his body convulsing as a result of his labored sobbing. The touch of my hand on his back set off an intense emotional eruption. He was crying so hard, I thought he might hurt himself. He was gasping for breath between the exhausting wrenches.

I waited several minutes to allow the bawling to subside. With my hand still on his back, I took a knee and leaned over to whisper into his ear, "I'm Chaplain Cook." Then I paused and pondered what to say. "God loves you, and I love you too." I felt a little uneasy about telling a man, a stranger no less, that I loved him but I also felt like it was the right thing to say. I continued, "You are obviously very upset and in a lot of pain. I care about you. How can I help?"

It took a few minutes for him to respond, but he blubbered, "I have messed up so bad," followed by a few more sobs. He finally turned his head towards the wall and I could see his chiseled jaw and a high-and-tight crew cut. He blurted out, "I can't believe that I screwed up my life like this."

After he calmed down a little, I prompted him to come into the counseling office and tell me his tragic story, which he seemed eager to do.

He told me he was a decorated Marine and that he had fought in the Kuwait and Iraqi wars. He said he had been discharged with honors about six months earlier and decided to settle in Los Angeles. He said that he picked up the tattoos and hooked up with his Blood brothers in LA. He told me that he was a cleaner, and that he was sent out by the gang on dirty business.

He began to cry again. "I have done so many... I can't... The horrible things I have done." He continued, "I can't believe I have hurt so many people... I have killed people... I am a trained killing machine."

Looking at his Hulk-like physique I could visualize his ability to inflict pain. I hesitated probing into this area for fear of discovering some felony or homicide. It was not clear to me whether he was referring to his past combat days or his present gang warfare.

Then he told me the events that led up to him finding the Airport Chapel. He and a set of Bloods had been out on some job. When they returned to the crib, they were all full of bravado.

He said, "I got cocky with the gang leader and in response he hit me with a bat. When I got up, I beat him almost to death. The other guys in the gang didn't look too happy with me, so I left to get a drink. I got word that the leader put a hit on me. I knew it was a death hit. So, I took what money I had and I bought a one way ticket to Atlanta on the next flight out. I got to Atlanta late last night and when I exited security I saw the Airport Chapel and I have been here all night. I got nowhere to go. God has left me."

I asked him, "Do you believe in God?"

He said, "I used to believe… My mom and dad are Christians… We used to go to church all the time back in Annapolis… I know they love me, but…" He began to cry again, only this time it wasn't from guilt. He was remembering LOVE.

He continued, "I love my dad, and when I joined the Marines, he was surprised. When I came home from Camp Lejeune, my dad was so proud of me… But I can't go back."

I remembered my own return home from basic training. I can remember walking up the driveway towards my waiting dad. I remember how much I wanted him to hug me and yes, even kiss me. It was and is one of the most important events of my life, and I can say, "Thank God, my father didn't let me down. He hugged me and he kissed me and he told me how proud he was of me. My mom also lavished me with her love."

"Why can't you go back?" I asked him.

He stuttered, "When I got back home from Iraq, I had a fight with my dad… I had a lot of stuff going on inside. I hit my Dad." He blurted out, "Something happened to me in Iraq… I forgot who I am... I lost my way and I can't go home." He looked up at the ceiling and said, "Jesus, can you help me?" He started to tear up again. He surprised me and leaned over on my shoulder and began to cry.

While he was crying on my shoulder, I whispered to him, "Why don't we pray and ask God to forgive us and help us find our way home?"

I prayed and he followed in short repeats. "Father, forgive me, help me find my way home to you and to my family…" At this point he began to pray of his own volition, "…I am so sorry Jesus, save me, save me, save me."

He didn't say any more, but the quiet presence of the Holy Spirit filled the room. I could sense in my spirit that God was doing a miraculous work in his spirit. The young man began to utter soft praises to the Lord, "Thank you, Jesus… Thank you, Jesus, Jesus, Jesus."

Then he looked at me full of a peace and joy that I recognized. And he hugged me. Ouch, did he hug me.

My spirit was also in a sacred celebration with his spirit. He was home. After a few minutes of deep breaths, I asked him "What is your name?" He said, "Jones, Sergeant Brian Jones."

Then I asked him, "What are your mom and dad's names? He told me their first names. I was already on the computer looking up their number on the internet.

He cautioned me, "I can't call them… I haven't spoken to them …" I interrupted with the phone in my hand. "I will call them and I will be the mediator."

The phone was ringing and a woman's voice answered. I introduced myself, "This is Chaplain Chester Cook at the Atlanta Airport and I have been talking to Brian…"

She Interrupted, "Brian? Is Brian with you? Is Brian there?"

I tried to answer her, "Yes Bri…" She interrupted, "Please, let me talk to him? Please?"

I held the phone out towards Brian and said, "I think it's your mother. She wants to talk to you."

I couldn't hear everything but I could tell that mom was very happy to hear his voice. I saw Brian begin to weep as he talked. Then, I heard what sounded to be his father's voice. It was an emotional moment. I could hear Brian say, "I love you too, dad and I am sorry."

While they talked, I checked online airfares, fearing the worst. But to my surprise, there were several flights that afternoon and the fares were around a hundred dollars. I asked Brian if I could speak to his parents. I asked them if Brian could come home for Christmas. To which they both replied, "YES!!! How wonderful."

I told them all that he would be home by dinner time on Christmas Eve, and booked the ticket.

Brian was home and was going home for Christmas.

CHAPTER FIVE

Love is Eternal

E the fourth letter of the acronym stands for,
Love is Eternal

Abraham Covenant:
"I will be their God...everlasting"
– Genesis 17:1-27

David Covenant:
"I will not take my steadfast love from him"
– II Samuel 7:14-15

"For a child is born to us, a son is given to us. And the government will rest on his shoulders. These will be his royal titles: Wonderful Counselor, and Mighty God, <u>Everlasting</u> Father, Prince of Peace. His ever expanding, peaceful government <u>will never end.</u>" – Isaiah 9:6-7

"Christ is the mediator of a new covenant, that those who are called may receive the promised <u>eternal</u> inheritance—now that he has died as a ransom to set them free from the sins committed under the first covenant." – Hebrews 9:15

"Keep yourselves in <u>God's love</u> as you wait for the mercy of our Lord Jesus Christ to bring you to <u>eternal</u> life." – Jude 1:21

God is eternal and God is love; therefore, love is eternal. Love is the means to the end and end to the means.

There is some question to the nature and essence of God in the Old Testament "The God of the Jews" and the New Testament "The God of the Christians." The image of God in the Torah has been described as retributive, wrathful and judgmental; while the God of the gospels is gracious, merciful and forgiving. The truth is the Love of God is covenantal and eternal towards the end.

To support this assertion I would like to use the passage of the Torah/Old Testament found in Exodus 33, 34.

Moses, the man to whom God revealed His name and the man who received the Ten Commandments, is also reported to be one of the few men to have ever been granted the privilege of seeing the glory of God. In Exodus 33:18 Moses said to God (YHWH), "Show me your glory."

In response to the request of Moses, in Exodus 34:9 God passed in front of Moses and proclaimed,

"The LORD, the LORD, the compassionate and gracious God, slow to anger, abounding in love and faithfulness, maintaining love to thousands, and forgiving wickedness, rebellion and sin. Yet he does not leave the guilty unpunished; he punishes the children and their children for the sin of the parents to the third and fourth generation."

The "abounding" Love of God was what Moses experienced when he encountered the manifest glory of God. God personified love. The "maintaining" Love of God sustains the universe, creation, and the beloved community.

> *"Love is greater than faith because the end is greater than the means. What is the purpose of having faith? It is to connect the soul with God. What is the object of connecting us with God? That we may become like God. But God is love. Thus the purpose of faith (the means) is so that we might love (the end). Love, therefore, is obviously greater than faith."*
> – Henry Drummond

The creative life giving Spirit continues to reproduce God's loving plan in creation by continuously working to sustain life and move towards consummation.

Why does this power of love in creation draw together the positive and the negative elements of the universe to bring life?

Theories of the origin of life fail to answer this question. Truthfully, this question can only be answered by the presence of a divine intelligence. The question is answered by the Divine Spirit of Love orchestrating the harmony and purpose of life. The Divine Spirit of Life causes all of the atoms of the universe to bring forth life and love.

Creation is a gift of God that connects all humanity. All humanity is systemically interconnected to creation through life. The fingerprint of God is in the beauty and complexity of creation. God's love is in the goodness of all creation.

The eternal promise is a shared love into eternity and a unification of love as our spirits depart this life and are united with the eternal Spirit of love.

> *"Man must evolve for all human conflict a method which rejects revenge, aggression and retaliation. The foundation of such a method is love."*
> – Martin Luther King Jr.

STORY SIX

Mrs. Mattie Mae McRae

People love my story about Mattie.

Early one morning, as I walked across the airport atrium, I saw an elderly black woman sitting on one of the comfy chairs near the elevator. She was dressed in a large sack dress, wearing glasses with thick "coke-bottle" lenses, clutching an oversized carpet bag, sitting with a metal orthopedic walker stationed in front of the chair. At first I thought she might be a homeless woman seeking refuge in the airport atrium but something triggered my chaplain senses.

I went up the elevator to the airport chapel, checked my morning e-mails and then set out to get my morning cup of Seattle's Best. I went back down the elevator and there she was still camped out in the chair. I passed by, smiled and said "good morning."

She replied, "good morning" with a frail English accent.

I retrieved my coffee and returned via the same route of encounter. As I approached the old woman I smiled at her and she smiled back. My radar was in alarm mode. I stopped and introduced myself and mentioned to her, "I noticed that you have been sitting in this same chair for over an hour and I wondered if there is anything I can do for you?"

She politely replied, "My name is Mattie Mae McRae and I am 81 years old. I went to a Church of God in Christ church conference in New Orleans but they had to evacuate us because of a hurricane. We just got off the bus and I am just waiting for my flight back to London."

I proceeded with my subsequent question, "Mrs. Mattie, when does your flight leave?"

She courteously replied, "Friday."

I was shocked because it was only Tuesday. I said, "Friday? Why Friday? Can't you get a flight out today?"

She said, "I asked the man at the ticket counter and he told me that my ticket absolutely, positively cannot be changed. So I'm gonna sit here till Friday, 'cus I don't have enough money for a hotel."

I was very confused and conflicted. I considered getting her a room for three nights but I thought I would see if she could get a flight out Tuesday afternoon. I secured a copy of her ticket and checked the Internet where I found that the flights to London for the next three days had hundreds of open seats. With my facts and ticket in hand I resolutely set out for the ticket counter.

I asked the ticket agent if I could get an earlier flight out that day. He typed for what seemed to be ten minutes and then handed me back the ticket and said, "This is one of those tickets that absolutely, positively cannot be changed."

I said, "What do you mean, 'This is one of those tickets that absolutely, positively cannot be changed?'" I continued, "It's a piece of paper."

He reiterated, "But sir, you don't understand. This is one of those tickets that absolutely, positively cannot be changed." He continued and said, "She could buy a new ticket for $2300.00."

I was a bit incensed by this time but held my righteous anger for another day. I said, "She already paid $1800.00 for the first ticket and should not have to pay for a second ticket." I remarked, "No wonder the airlines are going bankrupt."

He replied flippantly, "We are going broke because of people like this."

I volleyed back, "You could put Mrs. Mattie in one of the empty seats on today's flights, which will allow your airline to make $1800.00 on a seat that was about to takeoff as a non-revenue generating seat. You can turn right around and sell her seat on the

Friday flight, which is full, to another passenger trying to get home, and make an extra $2300.00." I politely said, "Thank you," and set off to find a supervisor.

I explained the whole story again to the supervisor, and after checking she informed me, "This is one of those tickets that absolutely, positively cannot be changed."

I sarcastically blurted out, "What idiot made up that policy?" She was not amused.

I decided that if something could be done only a Station Manager could authorize such a change. I found the Station Manager in his office and after a quick investigation he told me, "This is one of those tickets that absolutely, positively cannot be changed."

I chuckled and said, "I know, that's why I am here." I appealed to his humanitarian sagacity. I said to him, "If that was your 81 year old grandmother sitting out in the airport atrium you would be livid. I also bet that the local news would love to interview Mrs. Mattie."

He chuckled and said, "I'll get the ticket changed."

We became good friends and Mrs. Mattie got her ticket home. I had to pay a ticket change fee of $100.00 dollars, which seemed ridiculous but I was happy to pay it to get Mrs. Mattie home.

CHAPTER SIX

When Love is Crucified

"It was just before the Passover Feast. Jesus knew that the time had come for him to leave this world and go to the Father. Having loved his own who were in the world, he now showed them the full extent of his love." – John 13:1

As we look to the cross of Jesus it becomes a window into Heaven.

The shape of the cross forms the letter T.

The image identifies a primary principle of God in love and in our lives. As we look at the cross and go through life, we can hear the one question of God,

"DO YOU TRUST ME?"
T stands for TRUST.

PRINCIPLE ONE: TRUST IN LOVE

When Jesus looked at the cross he was confronted with the question from God, **"Do you trust Me?"** Even though Jesus understood the power of God beyond the cross, the cross was his ultimate test. Would Jesus go to the cross willingly believing that God could be trusted to resurrect him?

Could you trust God even unto death? How about trusting God to help you with your life? Your job? Your family? Your problem? Can God be trusted? The resurrection is proof that God can be trusted. God's love didn't let Jesus down and it won't let you down either.

God desires to be in our lives. This requires first, our recognition of His existence and a turning towards God, secondly, an acceptance of God's love and provision for reconciliation through the incarnation, death and resurrection of Jesus Christ, and thirdly, a life in pursuit of the Will of God towards the establishment of the Kingdom of Love.

Life is a spiritual boot camp to build faith into our lives. To have faith is to believe, trust, to put your whole weight upon. Paul says in Hebrews 11:1, "Faith is the substance of things hoped for the evidence of things not seen." When we look at a chair we hope that it will support us. As we sit we gain a trust in the substance of the chair. This substance now informs our experience and we begin to trust, not only the chair we sat in, but chairs in general. In time we don't think twice about sitting in chairs.

Peter says, "taste and know that the Lord is Good." 1 Peter 2:3 In much the same way God allows tests in our lives as a means of self-revelation. Test after test we begin to develop more and more trust (faith) in God. The test is not so we will fail, the test is to see us pass. The tests have ever increasing degrees of difficulty to increase our level of faith. The goal is to make us more competent in faith.

"Have faith in God. Truly I say to you, that whosoever shall say unto this mountain, be removed, and be cast into the sea; and shall not doubt in his heart, but shall believe that those things which he says shall come to pass; he shall have whatsoever he says." – Mark 11:23

What mountains are you facing?

"We know that God works in all things, for the good of those who love him, who have been called according to his purpose."
– Romans 8:28

From the time of Adam to Apocalypse, God asks,

"DO YOU TRUST ME?"

God required the same of Jesus and Adam that He requires of us; to trust (believe) God.

Trust is mandatory in any agape love relationship.

PRINCIPLE TWO: FAITH IN LOVE

"The only thing that matters is faith expressing itself through love." – Galatians 5:6

The importance of faith in love becomes clear when we begin to realize that love transforms the results. Faith without love is useless. Faith in love has divine and eternal significance. Faith in love is in harmony with God's intention; therefore, it is the Will of God.

Let me explain. The Will of God is synonymous with the Love of God. If God is Love then it is a reasonable conclusion that where the Love of God is present, the Will of God is present and vise versa.

Jesus abided in both the Love of God and Will of God; therefore, he could ask for whatever he needed. When we align our will to be in sync with the Love of God and the Will of God, we can pray for whatever is needed to accomplish the task. Jesus confirms this by saying, "whatever you ask for, in my name, you will receive." This verse directly precedes Jesus' command to love in John 15:7-9. Jesus links the believer's prayer to love. If you ask God to do something in my name (in the Love of God and the Will of God) the answer is already, Yes!

> *"Jesus believed in and trusted the Love of God."*
> – Chester Cook

When you pray do you pray for what God wants?
Or, do you pray for what you want?

James the brother of Jesus says, "You have not, because you ask with wrong motives, so that you can use what you get for your own agenda." James 4:3

The key to a successful prayer life is to pray in faith for what God wants. God is always ready to grant what God wants.

For starters, I would suggest praying to God about your situation and not providing your advice to God. Don't tell God how the prayer should be answered. Secondly, after you have prayed the prayer, leave it in God's hands. Trust in God's Love. God's Love will not fail. The answer God wants you to have will be provided in time and in love. If you pray, not my will but your will be done, you will get God's answer.

In time you will learn to walk in the Faith of God and Love of God and the Will of God. Your prayer will be in continuous expectation of God ministering simultaneously as you minister. Your Trust in God will be absolute. At this point God will use you to be a Kingdom of God builder.

If you begin this quest with the purpose of becoming somebody that others admire, you will never get off the launch pad. Please remember this is not about your ambition and agenda. This is not about becoming a somebody, a person of prestige and power. On the contrary, this is about becoming whoever God wants you to be. This is about becoming the unique perfect person that God created you to be.

PRINCIPLE THREE: GLORIFY IN LOVE

"I have glorified you on the earth:
I have finished the work that you gave me to do.
And now, O Father, glorify me with the glory
that I had with you before the world began." – John 17:5

Glorify is one of those heavenly words that has a difficult earthly definition. It is however one of the primary principals for living.

Once we have learned to trust God and love unconditionally we are faced with the day to day decisions of life. In life we are faced with decisions: turn left, turn right? Red or Blue? How are we to know which decision is the right one? Honestly, most of the time we don't know which decision is the right decision. We weigh out the outcome and we eliminate the bad choice and pick the good choice. But we still may be making the wrong decision. This is where glorify comes in. When we are faced with a decision we must apply principle one (faith) and two (love) and then as the Word of God instructs and the Spirit of God leads, make a decision that we honestly believe would be the Will of God. We make a decision that would please God.

> *"Do we sufficiently cultivate this unselfish desire to be all for JESUS, and to do all for His pleasure?*
>
> *Or are we conscious that we principally go to Him for our own sakes or at best for the sake of our fellow-creatures?*
> *How much of prayer there is that begins and ends with the creature, forgetful of the privilege of giving joy to the Creator! Yet it is only when He sees in our unselfish love and devotion to Him the reflection of His own that His heart can feel full satisfaction, and pour itself forth in precious utterances of love..."*
>
> *– Hudson Taylor True Love,* by Hudson Taylor
> Excerpts from "Union and Communion"

As we walk in the Faith of God and the Love of God, we are required to discern and do the Will of God. Jesus stated early in his ministry, "My sustenance is to do the will of Him who sent me and to finish His work." John 4:34 Again Jesus states, "For I came down from heaven, not to do mine own will, but the will of him that sent me." John 6:38 And finally in the Garden of Gethsemane Jesus prays, "Not my will but Your will be done." Luke 22:42

Simply put, our purpose is to do the Will of God and finish His work. As we minister in the name of Jesus in love, God is glorified in the believer, and in turn the believer is glorified by God.

"Jesus received honor and glory from God the Father when the voice came to him from the Majestic Glory, saying, 'This is my Son, whom I love; with him I am well pleased.'"
– 2 Peter 1:17

Jesus summed this up in a word, "glorify." To glorify is to reflect God and Jesus Christ in our life. We reflect God and Jesus Christ in our lives when others see our faith in God and our love for God as demonstrated through our love for others. God begins to glorify us as we glorify Him. The glorification of the believer is produced by the evidenced "Fruit of the Spirit" and the evidence of the "Gifts of the Holy Spirit" in operation.

When a believer is faced with a decision, the teachings of Jesus Christ and the Holy Spirit informs the follower to pursue the Will of God in the Love of God.

Is the situation you are praying about and ministering to, a situation where you are willing to accept the Will of God, no matter what?

Then pray and turn the outcome over to God. Be extremely careful not to try to fix the problem in your own way or strength. Don't hold on to the problem, give it to God and let it go. If you take the problem back through worry, doubt or self-reliance, then God will graciously give the problem back to you.

Is the situation you are praying about and ministering to, a situation where your motivation is love and you are believing that the Love of God will be evidenced in the answer?

Then remain in faith and expect love to prevail in the manifestation.

Is the situation you are praying about and ministering to, one where God will get all the glory?

Then believe, pray, let love prevail and God will answer, in such a way where no one can take credit (including doctors, ministers, and you). God gets all the glory. "And whatever you shall ask in my name, that will I do, that the Father may be glorified in the Son." John 14:13

Be very careful to stay out of the way and let God be the only one glorified. Realize that if you try to claim credit the answer will not come. God already knows if you will try to take the credit and you probably won't have any prayer or ministry success. You will probably be moved back to Start (like in the game called Life) and have to go through several more tests, over and over again. God will disciple (discipline) you until you learn these three simple lessons.

God desires that we operate in faith and love and that we walk in obedience and righteousness, which is another way of saying, walking in a way that pleases God. When we choose to trust, love and glorify, God can and will open and shut doors to guide us into his purpose and will.

TRUST - LOVE - GLORIFY
1. *Faith in God (trust)*
2. *Love as God Loves (love)*
3. *Glorify God [WWJD - please God] (glorify)*

UNILATERAL COMMITMENT

Sometimes in relationships love becomes so one sided that evil seizes the opportunity to inflict harm and even to crucify. The key is to stay the course of love. Don't let evil sidetrack you. In these situations you will need to stand on the Word of God as Jesus did in the Wilderness. In severe cases you may need divine intervention and

> *"I ain't gonna give up on love; love won't give up on me."*
> – Stevie Ray Vaughan

the protection of God to depart and avoid physical harm.

In the case of Jesus, he continued to openly invite everyone, even his enemies to be reconciled to God, by accepting his invitation to believe and follow after love. Jesus continued to be open and honest speaking the truth in love but his antagonist continued to look for any opportunity to kill him.

Evil was so calculated that it conspired, manipulated, lied and even fabricated evidence. In an effort to destroy Jesus and his movement of love, these so called religious people would do anything to bolster their power and maintain their dogmatic superiority. In an effort to defeat him they would repeatedly twist his words to malign his character. But Jesus would not retaliate. He would not strike back. He would not betray his essence or his message. He was resolutely determined to fulfill his Father's will. "As the time drew near for his return to heaven, Jesus resolutely set out for Jerusalem." Luke 9:51

The evil perpetrated upon Jesus by humanity, is recorded as the vilest act of evil ever inflicted upon an innocent man. His Father's call upon his life would ultimately be recorded as the most loving sacrifice in history. The **unilateral commitment** of love was offered even to those hammering the nails into his hands.

Jesus trusted God completely in life and now in death. Jesus loved God with all his heart, strength, soul and mind. And in a final show of his love for you and me, he laid down his life for you and me, so that we could be liberated from sin and reconciled to God.

"Greater love has no one than this, that he lay down his life for his friends." – John 15:3

Jesus glorified God in his life and death.

Jesus was willing to die for what he believed in.
JESUS BELIEVED IN LOVE.

Federal Witness Protection Program

The Atlanta airport atrium is situated in the center of the main terminal and is a beautiful window to the sky. The dome shaped glass canopy provides a panoramic picture of the planes flying overhead and the weather dejour. If you stand directly under the center cross of the crystal ceiling and say your name you can hear an architectural acoustic echo.

One day as I was walking across the atrium floor I saw two adolescent boys playing tag of some sort. I cautioned them about the horseplay and tried to redirect their energy to the bell effect sound of the atrium. I told one boy to stand on the X on the floor and say his name. He obliged and was pleased to hear his name echoed in the atrium air. He commandeered his brother to stand and speak and they both reveled in the acoustic ricochet.

Out of my peripheral vision, I viewed a woman ambushing me like a mother lioness protecting her cubs. I quickly realized her protective instinct at work and made a quick apology for not seeking her permission before speaking to them. She glared at me and saw my badge. Her stare went from suspicion to inquisition.

She said to me, "Can you help me find the FBI?"

She looked like a woman of high society. What we refer to in Atlanta as a "Dunwoody housewife". Her hair, jewelry and clothes all had a fashioned look; except for her shoes, she was wearing some strap sandals and her feet and toes were bloody. Her question and bloody toes caused me to be concerned that she might be in some serious trouble.

I apprehensively replied, "The FBI has offices in Atlanta and they have an officer assigned to the Airport but I will need to contact the ATL Police to have the FBI officer respond."

She grabbed my arm, "No she said, don't call the police. I can only talk to the FBI."

Now I was worried. What federal predicament was this woman entangled in?

She pulled me over and whispered in my ear, "I am in the witness relocation protection program and I am supposed to meet the officer here in the airport. They are going to relocate me and my children to Cancun." She grabbed her boys around the neck with her arms and pulled them close. The two boys rolled their eyes and fidgeted.

Was this woman a witness in a federal criminal case? Was someone trying to hunt her down to kill her? What was I getting myself involved in? I felt a sense of duty to help this woman find the FBI and fast.

"Where did the FBI tell you to meet them?" I asked.

She firmly replied, "The signs on the trucks were all codes from the FBI and they guided me to the airport."

Puzzled I responded, "Signs on the trucks?"

She continued, "Yes, I drove here from Tennessee two days ago and I parked my car in the government parking lot. I am supposed to fly out today. But where are they? I have to get to Cancun. Can you find them for me?"

One of the boys, still in half nelson, squeaked, "Can you help my mom?"

She squeezed his neck in her arm.

What did he mean, "Help my mom?" I sensed that he wasn't talking about finding the FBI. I redirected my questioning and asked her to come into the airport chapel office so I could call the FBI. She followed.

In the office one of the boys blurted out that he was hungry and the other boy nodded. I asked the mom if we could get them a hamburger and Frosty. She nonchalantly approved.

Deacon Don Kelsey went to get the kids a meal while I began to look in the chapel records and phone book for our FBI contact. When Don returned he motioned to me from the door. I could tell by his countenance that he had something important to say. I stuck my head out the door and he said that the oldest boy told him that they had not eaten in two days and that they had been walking the streets of Atlanta for two days. This explained why her feet were so bloody. I asked Don to sit with mom and I went into the outer room to talk to the boys.

At first the boys did not want to talk for fear that they would be getting their mom into trouble but after some assurance that I would be able to help her, they began to cry and share their love and concern for their mother. "My mom needs a doctor she is not feeling good. She took us out of school and we have been lost for three days. I will never get all my homework done."

I began to understand and reassured the boys that we would get their mother some help. Their mother was suffering from a schizophrenic illness. I asked the older boy if there was a father or grandparent I could call. He gave me the name of his grandparents in Tennessee.

I called the grandparents and the police to get the woman some help. The police took the woman and boys downtown until the grandparents arrived. It is my understanding that the children went home with their grandparents but the mother was released because she did not break any laws.

Mental illness is a serious problem in society and on any given day we encounter people with serious mental illness needs in the airport.

CHAPTER SEVEN

Be Love

As I wake in the morning
and set my feet on the floor beside my bed
I pray this simple prayer,

"God I love you!"
"Help me to love all that you love today!"
"Help me BE LOVE!"

"Be perfect, even as your Father in heaven is perfect."

– Matthew 5:48

BE PERFECT

World View – Perfection is often thought of as a goal to be achieved. The goal is some distant prize we may reach after years of striving and effort. This view is not obtainable.

Biblical View – Perfection is a state of completion, whole, lacking nothing. Shalom is a term that means peace. Peace is a place of perfect rest. Peace is the equivalent to perfection.

Musical notes are tuned to a certain frequency. In the case of the top string on a guitar, it is tuned to E.

$$E\flat < E < E\#$$

When the E string is tuned too loose it becomes Eflat when it is tuned too tight it becomes an Esharp (F). When it is perfectly tuned it is a perfectly pitched E.

In a similar way we are intended to be perfectly the person God created us to be. When we fail to be who we are created to be we are flat - when we strive to be more than who we are created to be we become sharp. God did not create me to be Moses, Jesus or anyone else; no, God created me to be me. God desires for me to be the perfect me – complete – whole – at peace.

Rev. John Wesley, the founder of the Methodist Church expressed this idea of "Christian Perfection" in his teachings and writings. Even against considerable theological criticism, Wesley held to this doctrine.

"(5.) This man can now testify to all mankind, 'I am crucified with Christ: Nevertheless I live; yet not I, but Christ liveth in me.' He is 'holy as God who called' him 'is holy,' both in heart and 'in all manner of conversation.' He 'loveth the Lord his God with all his heart,' and serveth him 'with all his strength.' He 'loveth his neighbour,' every man, 'as himself;' yea, 'as Christ loveth us;' them, in particular, that 'despitefully use him and persecute him, because they know not the Son, neither the Father.' Indeed his soul is all love, filled with 'bowels of mercies, kindness, meekness, gentleness, longsuffering.' And his life agreeth thereto, full of 'the work of faith, the patience of hope, the labour of love.' 'And whatsoever' he 'doeth either in word or deed,' he 'doeth it all in the name,' in the love and power, 'of the Lord Jesus.' In a word, he doeth 'the will of God on earth, as it is done in heaven.'

"(6.) This it is to be a perfect man, to be 'sanctified throughout;' even 'to have a heart so all-flaming with the love of God,' (to use Archbishop Usher's words,) 'as continually to offer up every

thought, word, and work, as a spiritual sacrifice, acceptable to God through Christ.' In every thought of our hearts, in every word of our tongues, in every work of our hands, to 'show forth his praise, who hath called us out of darkness into his marvellous light.' O that both we, and all who seek the Lord Jesus in sincerity, may thus 'be made perfect in one!'"
– John Wesley, *A Plain Account of Christian Perfection*

A perfectionist is someone who continually strives to be perfect - a perfect person is someone who is whole and only needs to be at rest. The name Noah in the Hebrew means rest.

Jesus speaks of being made "whole" – "healed" – "saved." He uses the same word "sozo" interchangeably. Additionally the idea of "righteousness," "holiness," and "perfectness" are all equal and imputed not merited.

"The whole point of being alive is to evolve into the complete person you were intended to be."
– Oprah Winfrey

The scriptures instruct the believer to "BE" what you are;

You are holy ▶ so be holy
You are righteous ▶ so be righteous
You are perfect (love) ▶ so be perfect (love)

"My dear, dear friends, if God loved us like this, we certainly ought to love each other. No one has seen God, ever. But if we love one another, God dwells deeply within us, and his love becomes complete in us—perfect love!"
– 1 John 4:12 (*The Message*)

Life is a journey for us to discover more of who we really are so that we can evolve to higher forms of expressing love until we can fully love unconditionally. Maturity is when we can fully allow the love of the divine to flow through us uninhibitedly.

BE HOLY

"Holy" is another one of those heavenly words that lacks a good human understanding and definition. Holy is replete in the Judeo-Christian scriptures and other religious texts but it is rarely used in common vocabulary. The word is best defined by its context in the Bible.

The Bible declares that "God is Holy." Most people are satisfied with this context. But when holy is used in reference to earthly contexts the comprehension is lost.

Holy regardless of context identifies the person, presence, perfection, purity, property and purpose of God.

In the Exodus story of Moses, God comes to Moses in the Burning Bush. God speaks to Moses and instructs him to remove his shoes because "the ground is holy."

What made the dirt holy?

The Tabernacle was a tent Moses setup in the desert. The tent was furnished with a table, altar and candlestick. These furnishings were consecrated as "holy..."

Why was the furniture holy?

Inside the Tabernacle was a curtain partitioning off the holiest Hebrew artifacts, the Arc of the Covenant. This space containing the Arc was called the "Holy of Holies."

What made this room the holiest place on earth?

To answer these questions we must know that holy is not a verb it is BE-ing. Be-ing holy is not an activity it is an attribute. The person of God is holy; the presence of God is holy; the perfection of God is holy; the purity of God is holy; the property of God is holy; the purpose of God is holy.

When we accept God:
God's Spirit presence unites with our spirit;
God's presence in us makes us perfect (holy).

God's Spirit in us purifies our spirit,
God's Spirit in us claims our spirit as His property,
God's Spirit in us activates our spirit for His purpose.

SELF-LOVE (ESTEEM)

Self-Love (Esteem) is the recognition and acknowledgement of our worth as a person. We are created and given our worth by God. It is important to begin with the understanding that our Heavenly Father's love is perfect. And that our Father perfectly loves each of us.

> *"Even the Bible tells us to 'love your neighbor as you love yourself.' You have to take care of yourself before you take care of anyone else."*
> – Phillip C. McGraw, Ph.D.

This self-esteem is affirmed by the love of our earthly mother and father. The failure of parents to provide love to a child results in poor self-esteem. Psychology books are full of complexes due to the absence of parental love or improper parental relationships. Many children suffer from low self-esteem and carry it into adult social relationships all because families fail to give proper love.

Some issues related to low self-esteem require professional help. The first step to recovery is to acknowledge a need for help. The second step is a desire to get better. Some people can't see their problem because they have repressed their trauma. Some recognize their problem but lack the will-power to rehabilitate. One way to recognize a need for help is to examine your social relationship with others.

<u>**Symptoms of poor self-esteem:**</u>
Bad relationship with our parents
Problems with our spouse
Troubles with our children
Difficulties with social relationships
Emotional problems

We all have an intrinsic need to be loved and a natural purpose to love. Whenever discrepancies are discovered in these instinctual needs, the capacity to love is diminished. Therefore, perfect love is not possible because the love tank is low.

You are never really free to love when you have issues that keep you from loving freely. You hold back from expressing love because of rejection, you hold back from expressing love because it is not reciprocated. When you allow yourself to love unconditionally, you are not afraid of rejection. You love fearlessly and freely without needing love in return. The most liberating kind of love is the carefree kind of love; it is the giving of yourself freely and not holding back.

> "We can only learn to love by loving."
> – Iris Murdoch

We all know how to give love, but sometimes we don't know how to receive love. If we are able to receive love as much as we are able to give it, we will complete the cycle of experiencing love with others for full happiness.

"Lord, make me an instrument of your peace.
Where there is hatred let me sow love;
where there is injury, pardon;
where there is doubt, faith;
where there is despair, hope;
where there is darkness, light;
where there is sadness, joy.

O Divine Master,
grant that I may not so much
seek to be consoled as to console;
to be understood as to understand;
to be loved as to love.

For it is in giving that we receive;

> *it is in pardoning that we are pardoned
> and it is in dying that we are born to eternal life."*
> – Saint Francis of Assisi

AUTHENTIC SELF

Be-ing love, Be-ing perfect, Be-ing holy are not orders to follow; rather, a status to be recognized. The King does not have to earn his position, he is the King but having the status and accepting its authority is a different challenge.

When the knowledge of position, and the integrity of character, are congruent authentic life emerges. The more we live in accordance with our authentic self before God, in Christ, the more fulfilled we will be.

As we live our lives we are confronted with events and choices that alter our perceptions of life and self. These external factors affect our internal thought process. The "marker events" in our life influence us both positively and negatively. Along the path our self-image can get distorted and damaged by events and experiences. Our psychological mind begins to feel like there are two people living within;

> *"No one can make you feel inferior without your consent."*
> – Eleanor Roosevelt

Fictional-self – the person that has been altered by all of the negative factors of life: distorted, weak, broken, lost, un-loved, un-loving .

Authentic-self – the being that is affirmed by the positive factors of life: competent, secure, strong, whole, safe, loved, loving.

The authentic person is the "Velveteen Rabbit" who has lived through the good and bad and evolved into a compassionate loving being, willing to be loved and to give love.

> *"Generally, by the time you are Real, most of your hair has been loved off, and your eyes drop out and you get all loose in the joints and very shabby. But these things don't matter at all, because once you are Real you can't be ugly, except to people who don't understand."*
> – Margery Williams, *The Velveteen Rabbit*

A person who is <u>self-differentiated</u> reaches a higher level of <u>actualization</u> and <u>consciousness</u>: three big words that refer to living up to your passion, purpose and potential.

You are in control of your now and future. Don't let others define and dictate your destiny. Don't let the external voices or your own internal voice dissuade your forward progress.

The double edged sword is: You can't change what you don't acknowledge but you can change what you do acknowledge. You can't change your past but you can choose how you respond to it. You may not be able to escape the consequences of your past actions or the harm that others have committed to you, but you can decide to start fresh. You have the choice to believe in yourself and to love yourself.

If after reading this book you still feel that you can't escape the trauma and consequence of your history, let me exhort you seek out help from a professional minister or doctor.

King-dom of God

The King Holiday honoring the legacy of Martin Luther King Jr. has become a virtual reality of the Kingdom of Love envisioned by Jesus.

I had the honor of being invited to offer the benediction at one of the Martin Luther King Jr. commemorative events in Atlanta. Many of the civil rights leaders were speaking from the podium that day and the one-hour event lasted well over four hours, which put my benediction very late into the day. I learned that some people liked church a lot more than others. By the time I said the benediction most of the crowd had already departed.

I have also had the privilege of having Martin Luther King III, speak at our IAC Annual Luncheon. While sitting next to him and discussing the world and culture of today, it was clear to me that our society has come a long way and has a long way to go.

Martin Luther King III spoke of a world where love ruled and reigned supreme. I so wanted the world to hear his words as he took the scriptural sayings of his father and made them his own. Like Elisha following in the footsteps of Elijah, Martin Luther King III was given a double portion of the Spirit to usher in the move of God.

When we all think back to the days of overt racism and then a few years later to the era of civil rights struggles it is disgraceful how "whites" behaved. It is even more appalling when I consider that most of those in power professed to be Christian.

I am happy to see the day honoring Martin Luther King Jr. evolve into a day of love and service to the "least of these"; a quote from Jesus in Matthew 25, "Then the King will say to those on his right, 'Come, you who are blessed by my Father; take your inheritance, the kingdom prepared for you since the creation of the world. For I was hungry and you gave me something to eat, I was thirsty and you gave me something to drink, I was a stranger and you invited me in, I needed clothes and you clothed me, I was sick and you looked after me, I was in prison and you came to visit me.'"

"Then the righteous will answer him, 'Lord, when did we see you hungry and feed you, or thirsty and give you something to drink? When did we see you a stranger and invite you in, or needing clothes and clothe you? When did we see you sick or in prison and go to visit you?'

"The King will reply, 'I tell you the truth, whatever you did for one of the least of these brothers of mine, you did for me.'"

I hope this King Day will find a way of continuing to actualize this parable. I pray that the saints will be ambassadors of love and reconciliation. I speak a word of faith with my brothers and sisters of the dream come true.

CHAPTER EIGHT

The Kingdom of Love

> *"If there's a lot of love in the world,*
> *there must be a lot of God in the world."*
> — Robert Schuler

"Neither shall they say, Lo here! or, lo there! for, behold,
the Kingdom of God is within you."
— Luke 17:21

Imagine a world where everyone loves like Jesus loved. Jesus came into our world to reveal this World of Love. Jesus lived as though this World of Love was already here. Jesus referred to this World as the Kingdom of God (Love). His command to love is at the heart of this Kingdom of Love. It is the only rule of this Kingdom of Love and the only duty of its subjects. Jesus died to usher in this Kingdom of Love.

> *"When I despair, I remember that all through history the ways*
> *of truth and love have always won. There have been tyrants, and*
> *murderers, and for a time they can seem invincible, but in the*
> *end they always fall. Think of it–always."* — Mahatma Ghandi

Is it possible to love God and to love Jesus Christ and not love what they love? The answer is obviously no. When we become a part of God's Kingdom of Love, the fine print in the contract includes loving all that God and Jesus love.

IS THIS WORLD OF LOVE POSSIBLE?

Hannah Hurnard was the daughter of Quaker parents. At age nineteen she struggled with thoughts of suicide. She lived with fear and humiliation because of her stammering speech. She had a hard time accepting the faith of her parents and the promises of the Bible. She saw the joy in the lives of other Christians but their joy only caused her more depression. During a holiness convention the speaker asked if anyone would like to offer a son or daughter for the mission field. Hannah's father placed his hand on her head and began to pray. Hannah wanted an answer from God so she opened her Bible where the pages fell upon the story of Elijah challenging the people of Israel to choose between Baal and the living God. God caused fire to fall on Elijah's sacrifice. Hannah believed that God was asking her to sacrifice her stammering lips for his use. "No, I can't do that," she said. "I would rather go straight to hell." Then she realized that she was already in her own personal hell. In the moments that followed, God revealed his love to her. Suddenly it seemed His very presence was in the room with her. "All I knew was that the Lord Jesus had come to me and made himself known to me in overwhelming love and glory and that all my heart went out to him, and I must follow hard after him." On July 26, 1924, about 1 p.m., Hannah found the joy of salvation. God took her stammer away.

Hannah answered the call to be a missionary. God sent her as a missionary to Jews, a people she initially disliked. She continued to feel God's love for herself but questioned why she did not feel love towards others. She used the image of an old rusty pump that needed manual effort. She however, wanted to be like the falls of Niagara with a continuous supply of love for others. Her desire was fulfilled when she received a Baptism of Holy Love from the Lord.

Hannah's story is much like many in ministry. She performed her missionary duties out of a sense of obligation. She felt called to bring people into the knowledge of salvation through doctrinal obedience. Her motivation was duty not love. Appealing to the doctrine of original sin, she justified her wrong attitude towards others. She felt that human nature was totally deprived. She writes, "All human beings were indeed very unpleasant creatures, with nothing naturally likable about them, full of faults and blemishes, as well as being capable of the most horrible sins and corruptions; that though God himself chose (for some mysterious reason) to love them, there was really nothing lovable about them, and that the Bible endorsed my own personal feelings that they were very unlikable indeed, and most of them would justly be outcast and condemned forever." Hannah began her missionary ministry feeling judgmental, critical and unloving towards the very people she was called to serve.

I too spent several years in ministry preaching from the pulpit and teaching from the Bible with some success. But I felt dry and often empty. I read Hannah's book, The Kingdom of Love, and realized I too needed to let love be the motivation behind ministry. I discovered what Hannah discovered, that love produces an everlasting fruit. It not only produces the fruit of joy in the minister it reproduces the fruit of miracles in the ministry.

I began to experience opportunities to share the Love of God with complete strangers. God saw the willingness of my heart to be a vessel of His love and divine encounters would spontaneously occur throughout the day. Through normal everyday conversations, people would inquire about spiritual issues and concerns. By counseling through love, the opportunity to also share Jesus Christ became possible. I found that people of every possible background, when loved, were receptive to the gospel offered in complete love. I never used a formula. I simply loved the person I was with, and shared with them the love that I have experienced through Jesus Christ.

I never used any coercive language when I spoke. The language of love softened their hearts, alleviated their fears and made their spirit receptive. I truly believe that the Holy Spirit of Love knew I could be trusted and offered me the privilege of experiencing one of the greatest joys; the joy of experiencing spiritual birth. I could not wait for the next love encounter. The spiritual experience of new birth was on the same level as the emotional experience of the birth of my own children.

Hannah offered a simple tool she called the ABC's of love as a way of learning to love as Christ loves.

1. **Love accepts – and loves all that God loves.**
2. **Love bears – all burdens in love.**
3. **Love creates – goodness through creative love.**

LOVE ACCEPTS

It seems intuitive that love would include the beloved. What God loves we should love. God loves the world so much that he gave his only begotten Son; therefore, we should love what God loves with the same sense of sacrifice. God has offered each of us the invitation to be a child of love in his family of love. This attitude puts us into the relationship of children in one large family, diverse in gifts and abilities and temperaments and vocations but all deeply interested in each other and lovingly ready to serve as the opportunity arises. It is also true that God hates sin; therefore, we must be careful to keep love holy.

> *"Love is not holy love until it becomes universal, that is to say, not love for some only, but love for all."*
> – William Law

LOVE BEARS

Love bears the burdens and disappointments of those we serve.

John the Baptist cried out "behold the lamb of God which beareth the sin of the world." John1:29 In this step of love we forbear the sin of others because we know that God loved us while we were yet sinners and that love covers a multitude of sins. Mother Teresa is an example of one who was willing to bear the burdens of the poorest children in India. Martin Luther King Jr. led the way as he marched bearing the injustices of prejudice and hatred on his back during the civil rights era in America, even unto death.

When we bear the burdens of others we provide love and support, when and where it is needed most. Jesus prayed on the cross as he bore the burdens of the world and prayed, "Father forgive them."

LOVE CREATES

Love creates goodness. The creative power of love always seeks to edify, encourage, and exhort. Love edifies and seeks to build others up. Love always encourages others to do better. Love exhorts others to reach their highest potential in Christ. Love calls fourth the God given goodness in every life. Just as Jesus called Peter "the rock" long before he was the finished product, love calls forth the diamond even while we are yet coal.

In this third step we must be very careful to do no harm. I have witnessed many Christians using the ways of the world in dealing with people. I have seen Christians crucify other Christians with their words and actions. I have seen ministers punished by their peers for common mistakes. And within the church I've witnessed hostilities that would make the Devil blush. Jesus said those who live by the sword will die by the sword. We cannot use the Devil's weapons in the Kingdom of Love.

> *"It may be true that the law cannot make a man love me,*
> *but it can stop him from lynching me,*
> *and I think that's pretty important."*
> – Martin Luther King Jr.

THE SPIRITUAL KINGDOM

Jesus explained to Pilate that his Kingdom was not of this world. The Kingdom Jesus referred to is a spiritual kingdom. The spiritual Kingdom of God begins in the heart when a believer allows the Spirit of God and the Love of God to rein. The Holy Spirit of Love then transforms the believer into the image of Christ.

We are the Kingdom of Love when we are subjects to the King of Love and allow his royal reign of love to rule in our hearts.

Love is the only prescription and remedy to the depraved human soul. Love is the only antidote to sin and love is the only eternal cure for our human condition.

It is not possible to love God without the provisions of Jesus Christ. For someone to say I love God but I do not believe in, or accept, Jesus Christ is ridiculous. One cannot be a lover of God and a disciple of love without including the Exemplar of Love, Jesus Christ. Any rejection of Jesus Christ is a rejection of perfect love and a rejection of God's invitation of love. When we accept Jesus Christ and his invitation of love we are making a commitment to love God and all that God loves. We are given the Christ Spirit and are indwelt with the Holy Spirit of God. We become one with God and Jesus Christ in the ultimate consummation of humanity. We become the beloved citizens of this new Community of Love. No one is permitted into this new Kingdom of Love without making a commitment to "be" love. To abide in love is to abide in God and in his love which includes abiding in Jesus Christ. This is the Christian life.

God created The Adamaic Kingdom (Adam) for fellowship. God walked with Adam in the Garden of Eden. God also made provisions for Adam to have love and companionship. God gave Adam complete freedom to partake in all the good that God had created. Adam was permitted to walk with God in perfect love. Adam was given a free will to respond in return to love - love must be free in order to be true - love must be given freely without coercion.

God gave Adam complete license over all of creation with one exception the tree which contained the fruit of the knowledge of evil. The tree containing the knowledge of evil would bring death to Adam and death to his spirit. The fruit of this tree contained the knowledge of evil that God was protecting Adam from the poison of evil. Every tree of the garden was good for Adam to enjoy. Adam could have lived with God in perfect communion if he had only trusted God's loving provision.

Adam chose not to trust God. Adam rejected God's love and experienced spiritual death. God was faced with three options:

1. The first option; God could offer complete forgiveness and restitution; this option was not possible because God's word stated that if Adam rejected God's loving provision and chose instead to consume the fruit from the tree containing the knowledge of evil he would suffer the consequences of death. Adam suffered the penalty.

2. The second option; God could destroy Adam in complete justice; but because God's love was still operating, God opted for justification.

3. The third option; God could provide a way of salvation for Adam and his seed, should they choose of their own free will to return to accept His atonement and His love. This salvation was made available by invitation through Jesus Christ.

God is love has always been pervasive towards Adam and his seed. But the way of salvation was established through the death of Jesus Christ. Jesus Christ removed the obstacle of sin through his sacrifice. Through Jesus Christ we are offered complete forgiveness and reconciliation. Jesus is the open invitation to anyone, who will of their own free will, return to the God of love.

"Nothing takes the taste out of peanut butter quite like unrequited love."
– Charlie Brown, *Peanuts* by Charles M. Schulz

STORY NINE

O Danny Boy

"My only option is deportation. I'll have to let them deport me."

Deportation can be a serious offence. It is one form of travel that most people never have to consider. But Gordon was at the end of his rainbow and someone had stolen his pot of gold.

Gordon possessed a student visa and had just finished a summer internship with a large beverage company here in Atlanta. He used a pre-paid credit card as his primary form of currency and had planned to use it one final time to purchase his ticket to Edinburg, Scotland. He was to start a new job on the following Monday when he returned to Scotland.

Gordon was a young man with short red hair, and a ruddy completion. He was very friendly with preppy fashion apparel. I gathered that he was here in Atlanta as a college exchange student working on an internship with Coca Cola. He was a very intelligent and had a genuinely friendly and likeable personality. He had all of his belongings packed neatly into his suitcase and a backpack, and was well prepared for his trip home. A friend dropped him off at a MARTA station to make his final trek to the airport. He had every detail worked out and his plan was meticulous but it did not include a contingency plan. He had not planned on someone stealing his wallet.

Gordon was sitting in the chapel and was not able to think very straight. He told us that he had $1800.00 dollars on the pre-paid credit card and he even had a bank receipt in his front pocket from that morning that verified this truth. Gordon was not asking for any assistance he was just trying to figure what to do. I listened to his story and told him to get with his friends in Atlanta to see if they could help him get the ticket home. Gordon called a couple of his friends and left resolved to work it out.

Three days later I walked into the Airport Chapel and Gordon had returned. He was very depressed and said that his friends in Atlanta did not have enough money and his time was running out. He said that he only had two days left on his visa and that he was going to turn himself into immigration and get deported. He said that if he got deported he would not be able to enter the United States for ten years.

I had concerns about fines, incarceration and detainment. I did find out that the process sometimes takes months where the deportee is held in a jail like facility for 30 to 60 days pending a hearing and deportation.

By this time we had had several hours together with Gordon and found him to be one of the nicest young men we had ever counseled. He never asked for a dime of help.

We took Gordon to lunch and found out that he was a good Christian boy and that he was going to work for a beverage distributor when he returned home. He felt sure that his job would be lost because he would not be there on Monday. Before we ate we said a prayer of thanks for the food and lifted Gordon's dilemma to the Divine deliverer.

After lunch I felt compelled to check on some possibilities. I asked Gordon if we could get him to London, England could he get a family member or friend to pick him up. He was willing to give this a try.

I went online and I found a ticket to London for $1200.00, ouch. But when I tried ATL to EDI I could not believe my eyes, $275.00. I thought I put in the wrong code.

I looked at Gordon and said "Oh Danny boy the pipes the pipes are call'in"

He said to me, "Chaplain Cook that's an Irish song and I am from Scotland."

I said, "You will have to show me around Scotland one day. Would you like to go home to Scotland tonight?"

He looked at me and rubbed his red hair and said, "Yes, but how?"

I said, "The Lord answered our prayer and you will be home on Sunday morning just in time for church."

Gordon wrote Ben DeCosta, The ATL General Manager, the nicest letter of appreciation resulting in a SHINNING STAR award.

CHAPTER NINE

John on Love

THE BELOVED DISCIPLE

I know I am not supposed to be biased but I love John. (John the evangelist, the beloved) (Not to be confused with John the Baptist)

John was one of the first men to meet and follow Jesus. He was there at the beginning when Jesus answered his call.

John was present when Jesus was baptized, at the Sermon on the Mount, on the Mountain of Transfiguration, at the Passover (last supper), in the Garden of Gethsemane, at the cross, and at the empty tomb.

John was so beloved and trusted that Jesus granted him the care of his mother, Mary, upon his death at Calvary.

"One of them, the disciple whom Jesus loved (John), was reclining next to him."
— John 13:23

"When Jesus saw his mother there, and the disciple whom he loved (John) standing nearby, he said to his mother, 'Dear woman, here is your son,'" – John 19:26

"So she came running to Simon Peter and the other disciple, the one Jesus loved (John), and said, 'They have taken the Lord out of the tomb, and we don't know where they have put him!'"
– John 20:2

"Then the disciple whom Jesus loved (John) said to Peter, 'It is the Lord!'"
– John 21:7

John was very intimate with Jesus and was referred to as the "beloved" disciple. He was part of the intimate inner circle of three (Peter, James and John).

John witnessed the life, teachings, miracles and love of Jesus first hand and he wrote first hand in the gospel account that bears his name: The Gospel of John.

JOHN'S GOSPEL

John is credited with the most frequently quoted scripture of all time,

"For God so loved the world that He gave his one and only Son, that whoever believes in him shall not perish but have eternal life."
– John 3:16

In this verse, God so loved the world, John immediately lays a foundation of God's love for all humanity (creation). John proclaims that God loves the "WORLD". The world is every living soul that has ever existed on this green Earth. God's love (agape) is universal, unchanging, and unconditional. The extreme extent of God's love was demonstrated in the supremacy of his commitment to give Jesus Christ as a means of reestablishing communion through belief. Jesus is an invitation of love to accept.

Jesus teaches that God loves the world. God loves the entire world not just a privileged few or a pious sect. Yes, God loves the entire world, even the undeserving. God does not say, "I will love you if, or when, or but." God does not say "I will love you if you love me," or "when you change." God's word declares, God has already vowed to love us. Please keep in mind love is a covenantal relationship; those who choose to live in the relationship benefit from its covenant, those who choose to reject the covenant decline its contractual privileges.

> *"God proved His love on the cross. When Christ hung, and bled, and died, it was God saying to the world, 'I love you.'"*
> – Billy Graham

The next offer is to "whosoever." Whoever, anyone, that desires to be in a love relationship with God, needs only to turn to, accept, receive, believe and surrender to God's invitation.

Rejecting God's invitation of love is paramount to rejecting God, love and life - (nihilation - voluntary separation from God - death). When people reject God, Jesus Christ or love, I question what they are offering as an alternative? What is the alternative to love?

Rejecting Jesus is also paramount to rejecting love. How can we say we believe in love and not include a person of perfect love.

THE FATHER AND SON - ONE IN LOVE

John describes a Jesus who opposes the human conception of an impersonal unloving God. John reveals Jesus and God in a special Father and Son relationship.

> *"The Father loves the Son and has placed everything in his hands."*
> – John 3:35

"For the Father loves the Son and shows him all he does."
— John 5:20
*"No, the Father himself loves you because you have
loved me and have believed that I came from God."*
— John 17:23
*"I in them and you in me. May they be brought to complete unity
to let the world know that you sent me and have loved them even
as you have loved me."* — John 17:24

Jesus imparts a conception of God as Daddy, "Abba". God was his Father. Scot McKnight in his book, The Jesus Creed, does a good job of communicating the intimacy of understanding God as our Father, "in Abba Jesus chooses a term from home because love originates in a home where an Abba dwells."(McKnight, p. 26) Jesus further alliterates that God is like a father who gives good gifts to his children. For Jesus, God was living and personal, with the desire of a father for his child. God loves and desires to be in a loving relationship with the beloved. Jesus Christ knew the Love of God in a very personal and intimate way.

John extends this intimate family relationship to those who will believe. The invitation to be a child of God is offered in love to anyone, everyone, all who will believe.

*"To all who did receive him (Jesus/God), to those who believed
in his name, he gave the right to become children of God -
children born not of natural descent, nor of human decision or a
husband's will, but born of God."* — John 1:12-13

Jesus experienced a loving God in the daily enjoyment of life and found that he could be in harmony with God and creation through being one with God in nature and purpose.

JOHN REVEALS THE IDENTITY OF JESUS

John's best-friend friendship with Jesus provides clear

identification of the identity and purpose of Jesus. John does not want there to be any question or doubt about Jesus' claim of Divine origin or his messianic salvation of the world.

"Very truly I tell you," Jesus answered, "before Abraham was born, I AM!" – John 8:58

In the Gospel of John, Jesus is depicted as the "I Am" and is quoted using this name for himself to assert his Divinity. The name "I Am" (Hebrew: YHWH)(Greek: ego eimi) is the same name that was spoken to Moses at the burning bush when Moses asked God to tell him His name, Exodus 4:14. John supports Jesus' claim by capturing Jesus' profound teachings and miraculous miracles. Jesus is ultimately accused of blasphemy and brought before the Roman Governor Pontius Pilate, because he claimed that he was the "Son of God." Pilate turned Jesus over to be scourged and crucified for this offence.

"We are not stoning you for any good work," they replied, "but for blasphemy, because you, a mere man, claim to be God… Why then do you accuse me of blasphemy because I said, 'I am God's Son'? Do not believe me unless I do the works of my Father. But if I do them, even though you do not believe me, believe the works, that you may know and understand that the Father is in me, and I in the Father." – John 10:33-38

The Father of Love incarnate in the Son of Love provides ample proof of divine power through the means of good works, miracles, forgiveness of sin power over nature and power over death. Jesus announces to the world that he has the power to resurrect and give life to all who believe.

"Jesus said to her, "I AM the resurrection and the life. The one who believes in me will live, even though they die; and whoever lives by believing in me will never die. Do you believe this?" "Yes, Lord," she replied, "I believe that you are the Messiah, the Son of God, who is to come into the world." – John 11:25-27

The final act of the Christ/Messiah, the Son of God is to be the savior of the world and to eradicate to power of sin and death. Jesus the first to be resurrected becomes the gateway to the Kingdom of Love for eternity.

"I have made you known to them, and will continue to make you known in order that the love you have for me may be in them and that I myself may be in them."
— John 17:26

Jesus Challenges Peter in Love (Agape)

"When they had finished eating, Jesus said to Simon Peter, "Simon son of John, do you love (agape) *me more than these?"*
"Yes, Lord," he said, "you know that I love (phileo) *you."*
Jesus said, "Feed my lambs."
Again Jesus said, "Simon son of John, do you love (agape) *me?"*
He answered, "Yes, Lord, you know that I love (phileo) *you."*
Jesus said, "Take care of my sheep."
The third time he said to him, "Simon son of John, do you love (phileo) *me?" Peter was hurt because Jesus asked him the third time, "Do you love* (phileo) *me?" He said, "Lord, you know all things; you know that I love* (phileo) *you."*
Jesus said, "Feed my sheep." — John 21:15-17

The disciple John, records a post-resurrection conversation between Jesus and Peter, the disciple that Jesus was grooming to be a leader of the church. There are many lessons to be learned in this encounter but the primary lesson that I would like to explore is the use of the word love, agape and phileo. If we read carefully we quickly see that Jesus is asking Peter "Do you love (agape) me?" but the humbled Peter can only muster "You know that I love (phileo) you."

The lesson we need to learn is that Jesus Christ requires love (agape) of his followers. All believers are challenged to evolve from phileo into agape.

THE LETTERS OF JOHN I, II, III
"God is Love"

John's letters to the first century church were written to address certain schools of heretical teachings that were infiltrating and corrupting the fundamental doctrines of the apostolic community.

In these three short letters, the word "love" appears 48 times in 34 verses. John emphasizes three primary beliefs that characterize the core Christian catechism.

1. Jesus Christ was the Son of God (incarnate).

2. Those who believe in the Son of God will have eternal life.

3. God is Love and you will know a Christian by their love.

I personally feel that new Christians should begin their Christianity 101 lesson by reading the first letter of John.

Rather than making expository commentary on John's teachings I would like to let you read selected passages for yourself.

"Dear friends, let us love one another, for love comes from God. Everyone who loves has been born of God and knows God. Whoever does not love does not know God, because God is love. This is how God showed his love among us: He sent his one and only Son into the world that we might live through him. This is love: not that we loved God, but that he loved us and sent his Son as an atoning sacrifice for our sins. Dear friends, since God so loved us, we also ought to love one another. No one has ever seen God; but if we love one another, God lives in us and his love is made complete in us. This is how we know that we live in him and he in us: He has given us of his Spirit. And we have seen and testify that the Father has sent his Son to be the Savior of the world. If anyone acknowledges that Jesus is the Son of God, God lives in them and they in God. And so we know and rely on the love God has for us. God is love. Whoever lives in love lives in God, and God in them. This

is how love is made complete among us so that we will have confidence on the day of judgment: In this world we are like Jesus. There is no fear in love. But perfect love drives out fear, because fear has to do with punishment. The one who fears is not made perfect in love. We love because he first loved us. Whoever claims to love God yet hates a brother or sister is a liar. For whoever does not love their brother and sister, whom they have seen, cannot love God, whom they have not seen. And he has given us this command: Anyone who loves God must also love their brother and sister."

– 1 John 4:7-21

The Girl from Ipanema

Cowering in the chapel library was a woman, a young girl with her head covered by a blue silk scarf; it was covering her face and was pulled diagonally to one side so as to cover only one eye. She was wearing a dark blue velour jogging suit, like a velvet painting, with beautiful hair flowing down her back, very long and brown, thick like a horse's tail but soft and smooth.

She had her back to me and at first I thought she might be a Muslim woman who was attending to her daily prayer. She had a ragged carry on flight bag and a piece of checked luggage that looked like it weighed a ton.

When she saw me out of the corner of her eye she recoiled towards the darkness of the room. I felt that her repel implied that she did not want to be seen or engaged into a conversation, so I walked past her into the chapel office. I sensed something was wrong.

I picked up a few devotional books to restock the front reception table knowing that this activity would bring my path back into the proximity of the library. As I walked past the door I could hear soft weeping. I put the devotionals into the display.

She must have heard my deliberate clatter because she stopped weeping and turned towards the door. She warily asked me if I would watch her bag.

Bag watching is a serious no-no for the chapel. Airline policy and the Transportation Security Authority (TSA) require that passengers be in possession of their bags at all time.

I wanted to help her and I did not want to tell her no, so I asked her why she needed to leave her bag. As she showed me her bandaged wrist she informed me that she wanted to go to the restroom and that her right arm was badly injured. She said it was difficult to pull the heavy bag around.

She turned towards me and the overhead light struck her face and reflected off her bronze skin. I noticed some swelling and purple bruising around her lips. I asked her if she needed medical attention. Immediately, she winced and became anxious. I surrendered questioning and said, "You are obviously in a lot of pain. I will help you any way I can."

She looked as though she wanted to believe but I determined that her "trust" was also injured. I calmly and caringly said to her, "You're safe here, I promise."

Cautiously re-engaging eye contact, she pulled back the blue veil on her face. I was stunned not only by her natural beauty but also by the violent damage inflicted to the right side of her face. Grotesque whelps of red, black, purple and green disfigured her eyes, nose and cheeks.

She told me her name was Maria and began to reveal to me a series of tragic events that brought her to the Airport Chapel. She told me that she was a hospital medical worker in New York. She said that a doctor at the hospital where she worked raped her. When she reported the rape to the hospital authorities, they informed her that the matter would be investigated. A couple of days later she was notified by the hospital that she was being terminated. She went to the State and tried to get some justice but they also sided with the hospital.

Young, scared, broke and alone she took her last dollars and purchased a one way ticket on a discount airline, to her home, Rio de Janeiro. She got a room near the Newark airport and decided to get dinner. On the way to dinner two women hanging out on the street attacked her, beat her into unconsciousness and stole her necklaces, rings and purse. She was treated at an emergency room in New York and released. In her injured condition she boarded her flight to Rio via Atlanta.

Once she arrived in Atlanta her tragedy went from bad to worse, her discount airline lost her luggage and failed to check her in on time; to add insult to injury they wanted to charge her a $100 ticket change fee. I offered to revisit the ticket counter and told her to bring her checked bag. Along the way she paid a visit to the ladies restroom.

After a little confrontation at the ticket counter I realized that arguing with the ticket agent was pointless. We assisted Maria with the ticket change fee and she was re-ticketed for the 6:00 a.m. flight the following morning. In order for her to check her bag she needed to be in line at 4:00 a.m. I agreed to let her stay in the chapel library. Upon leaving I said a prayer with her and gave her a key that she could use to lock the library door and rest.

At 1:00 a.m. my phone rang and it was the airport police. They found Maria in the library room and demanded that she open the door. In her paranoid state she refused and the police used a master key to get the door open. They were going to lock her up but I pleaded with them to understand her situation. Thankfully, one of the CIT (critical incident trained) officers intervened and said "If Chaplain Cook was trying to help her, we should also help her."

Thank God, Maria made her flight. I occasionally think of her and pray for her. I am also grieved that her experience of the United States was so tragically un-loving.

CHAPTER TEN

Paul on Love

Saul was a Jewish contemporary of Jesus. His knowledge of God was formed by strict training and adherence to Jewish Law. Saul viewed himself as a "righteous" man and an orthodox rabbinic Jew. His mission in life was to seek out followers of Jesus and kill them. In many ways Saul was practicing a form of "jihad" and genocide. In his own warped mind Saul had formed an image of God that was exclusive, condemning and punitive. Saul however went through a radical transformation of being and character, when he was converted on the Damascus Road (Acts 11) and his name was changed to Paul. The bounty hunting ministry of Paul, the Jewish elitist, did a 180 degree turn and Paul became a follower of Jesus Christ and the "Apostle to the Gentiles."

The writings of Paul now comprise over a third of the Christian scriptures contained in the New Testament. Paul is credited with composing some of the most practical and influential words about love ever written, including his address on love in his letter to the church at Rome, Corinth Galatia, Ephesus, Philippi, Colosse, and Thessalonica.

Paul has much to say on a variety of topics. I will try to confine this commentary to his teachings on what he refers to as the "greatest of these," love.

ROMANS

Paul exhorted the church at Rome with the central practical message believe in Christ, walk in the Spirit and love.

Paul's letter to Rome states that all people have sinned towards God; but, God offers forgiveness and reconciliation through the grace of God in Jesus Christ and that by faith in Jesus Christ believers are given eternal life by the indwelling of the Spirit.

"Therefore, since we have been justified through faith, we have peace with God through our Lord Jesus Christ, through whom we have gained access by faith into this grace... God has poured out his love into our hearts by the Holy Spirit, whom he has given us." – Romans 5:1-5

Paul further confirms that the Holy Spirit confers spiritual life and power to the believer to live for Christ. Spirit is perfect, complete and whole. Spirit does not need anything to define what it is. It already has everything it wants and is everything it wants to be. The Christian believer full of the Holy Spirit is a vessel filled with the Love of God.

The Law of the Spirit is greater than the Law of Sin. Both are always on the table but the Law of the Spirit always trumps the Law of Sin. Feed the Spirit and exercise the Spirit and it will become stronger while the flesh will starve and becomes faint. The stronger Spirit will always bring forth the fruit of love.

"Who shall separate us from the love of Christ? Shall trouble or hardship or persecution or famine or nakedness or danger or sword?" – Romans 8:35
"Neither height nor depth, nor anything else in all creation, will be able to separate us from the love of God that is in Christ Jesus our Lord." – Romans 8:39
"Love must be sincere...Be devoted to one another in brotherly love." – Romans 12:9-10

The apostle Paul asserts that nothing will ever be able to separate us from the Love of God and the Love of Christ. Love once received conjoins the believer into the beloved and provides eternal security. Love conjoins believers into one devoted community. The community of followers is obligated to love.

Paul advocates that we should love our neighbors as we love ourselves. I would add that we should love others as we love Jesus Christ himself.

Paul further states that "love does no harm to his neighbor." At first read this phrase seems simple enough but when we think of our own conduct, speech and transgression towards others we soon realize how far from love we truly are. It is wrong to steal

> *"I have found the paradox that if I love until it hurts, then there is no hurt, but only more love."*
> – Mother Teresa

or kill but it is just as wrong to be unloving towards someone. One sinful act towards another person is a violation of love. One unkind word towards another person is a violation of love. One selfish act in business, at church, or at home, is a violation of love.

> *"Owe no one anything except to love one another, for he who loves another has fulfilled the law. For the commandments, "You shall not commit adultery," "You shall not murder," "You shall not steal," "You shall not bear false witness," "You shall not covet," and if there is any other commandment, are all summed up in this saying, namely, you shall love your neighbor as yourself. Love does <u>no harm</u> to a neighbor; therefore, love is the <u>fulfillment</u> of the law."* – Romans 13:8-10

The goal of keeping a checklist of rules, a code of conduct, or even the Ten Commandments is frivolous. Love is the actualization of perfect conduct. In loving others we fulfill all of God's law. Paul states that if we love someone we would not want to hurt them in any way; therefore, the obligation of the Ten Commandments is fulfilled by the superiority of love.

To be love we must consider all of our actions and words towards others. We must seek to be what we are: Be love.

CORINTHIANS

Paul's letter to the Church at Corinth was written to help the believers live for Christ in the midst of a corrupt society. In this letter Paul addresses several issues in the church and offers solutions. Paul offers a supreme solution found in what is commonly referred to as the "Love Chapter."

> *"The one great need in our Christian life is love, more love to God and to each other. Would that we could all move into Paul's chapter, and lived there."*
>
> – D.L. Moody
> [*The Greatest Thing in the World*, Henry Drummond (p. 3)]

I CORINTHIANS 13 – THE LOVE CHAPTER

"Though I speak with the tongues of men and of angels, but have not love, I have become sounding brass or a clanging cymbal.

And though I have the gift of prophecy, and understand all mysteries and all knowledge, and though I have all faith, so that I could remove mountains, but have not love, I am nothing.

And though I bestow all my goods to feed the poor, and though I give my body to be burned, but have not love, it profits me nothing.

Love is patient

Love is kind;

Love does not envy

Love does not boast

Love is not proud

Love is not rude

Love is not self seeking

Love is not easily angered

Love keeps no record of wrongs

Love does not delight in evil

Love rejoices with the truth

Love always protects

Love always trust

Love always perseveres

Love never fails

But whether there are prophecies, they will fail; whether there are tongues, they will cease; whether there is knowledge, it will vanish away. For we know in part and we prophesy in part. But when that which is perfect has come, then that which is in part will be done away. When I was a child, I spoke as a child, I understood as a child, I thought as a child; but when I became a man, I put away childish things. For now we see in a mirror, dimly, but then face to face. Now I know in part, but then I shall know just as I also am known.

And now abide faith, hope, love, these three; but the greatest of these is love."

CHARITY (LOVE)

In the King James translation of this "Love Chapter" the Greek word agape is translated "charity." By translating agape as charity the reader is made aware of the divine giving attribute of love.

"Remember, LOVE is the greatest thing, and it is all that will last in eternity. Choose to establish yourself in love and let it be firm within you."
– Joel Osteen

Paul's list of love descriptors provides a good checklist to use to evaluate agape (love) in practical living.

I recommend memorizing Corinthians chapter 13. According to Paul the attributes of LOVE are:

LOVE is PATIENT. As a Christian in the love (agape) business, I can vouch for the necessity of patience when dealing with life and people. As a father I must be patient with my children to allow them the time to mature. In much the same way as Christians we must be patient with each other to allow love to mature. It is not easy because we have to put up with carnality and ignorance, but the goal is the discipleship and love. It is well worth it !!

LOVE is KIND. How sweet is the thoughtful kindness of Love. The gentle softness of a word or a gesture creates a warmth of relationship and fosters an intimacy of trust. Love grows in the kind honoring of a mother or father, the kind parenting of children, the kind consideration of a friendship and the kind caring for our beloved in a relationship. When we get love attribute #1 and #2 buttoned in the right order, the other buttons begin to line up. God is kind. God help me be kind, not just to the deserving but to even to the rude. "A kind word turns away wrath."

LOVE does not ENVY (COVET). How hard it is, not to want. Covet, envy, jealousy are all a lack of contentment with what God has already given. This does not mean we shouldn't set goals or have dreams - It means that it is harmful when we make a comparison of our life/stuff with the life/stuff of others. Thou shall not covet is the Tenth Commandment and is a catch-all. There are Nine "concise" commandments and then Ten is "everything else." God gives us everything we need and deserve. We should want what God wants. If you want more - Ask God what He wants and then put your hand to the plow. What do you want?

LOVE does not BOAST. Boasting is the opposite of humility. Boasting leaves an arrogant aftertaste that degrades others. Again, bragging is self-centered and not sensitive about the care of others. Give God the glory for your blessings and share your good fortune with others without any need for reward or self-aggrandizement.

LOVE is not PROUD. The psalmist says, "Pride goes before a fall." Lucifer's pride: "For thou hast said in thine heart, I will ascend into heaven, I will exalt my throne above the stars of God:" Pride is a vice that is hard to root out, even in the most committed Christian. It is one thing to stop stealing - but to clean out PRIDE it takes a baptism of love. Love desires the well-being of others - not selfish egotistical glorification. Focus on glorifying God and let God glorify you. Jesus said, "I glorify my Father, He glorifies me."

LOVE is not RUDE. Love has a social maturity that values relationships. Social behavior should encourage the strengthening of individual civil trust. Anti-social behaviors like bullying, obscenity, profanity, lewdness, ethnic slurs, hate speech, nose picking, yelling and a whole list of impolite activities are all violations. While mature Christians may graciously forgive improper behavior we must be careful not to be rude to rude people; but to instruct towards maturity. This is where Paul exhorts; "We who are strong have an obligation to bear with the failings of the weak, and not to please ourselves." Romans 15:1 We all have room to clean up our act a little bit especially with those we live with on a day to day basis.

LOVE is not SELF SEEKING. This King James rendering of love as "charity" helps the reader understand love's definition and direction: Giving. Love extends service in the direction of the needy. Love is a commitment of the will for the well-being of others. Love is not coercive or demanding. Love does not seek its own way; rather, it is invitational. The KINGDOM of LOVE includes all who accept this invitation of God's Love and by necessity includes Jesus Christ who is the epitome of love.

LOVE is not easily ANGERED. Anger is an emotion that allows us to let off some steam. Some people internalize their anger and implode; while others externalize their anger and explode. The key to anger is to maintain control so as to channel the steam of anger into small therapeutic doses, like a pressure valve. Another valued approach is to re-channel the steam of anger into productive activity or personal edification. Remember the admonition about anger, "In your anger do not sin."

LOVE thinks no EVIL (keeps no record of WRONGS). The New International Version translates this verse, "Love... keeps no record of wrong." Even though it is hard to do, I have tried to erase my hard-drive of debtors. No good can come from thoughts of retribution or evil planning. If you have been hurt, forgive, forget and give them to the Lord. Let the Lord be your mediator. Love focuses on thoughts of doing good.

LOVE does not delight in EVIL. Not only does love not think evil, it can't stand the sight of evil. Love desires the "Fruit of the Spirit" Galatians 5:22, and deplores the un-righteous activities of evil. Love seeks to make right the injustices of this life. Love prays, "Deliver us from evil." Feed good and starve evil. In this way Love will get stronger and evil will surly die.

LOVE rejoices in the TRUTH. Truth is as real as it gets. When the truth is found it trumps all other dialogue or idea. Because truth is fact it can stand all scrutiny and still prevail. Love wants the truth the whole truth and nothing but the truth. Any attempt to lie in the shadows reveals deception. The truth will set you free. Many of the world problems and our personal problems are created because we fail to operate in truth.

LOVE always PROTECTS. Security is a basic human need. The fiduciary duty of love is to guard, defend and protect as a lawyer does for a client. Like a mother defending her young, ultimately love lays down its life to save the life of the beloved.

LOVE always TRUSTS. When we entrust ourselves to another we are placing our trust in their fidelity. Love will never betray this entrustment. Trust in love is the strongest bond in the world. Love is the anchor moored in heavens promise.

LOVE always PERSEVERES. Love never gives up or quits. It continues the quest when others retire. Love maintains the search when others leave. Love is the voice saying, I knew you would come. Love apprehends the promise of God's Word.

LOVE never FAILS. Love holds the promise of God that any activity motivated by love will succeed. It will not fail. Love is the divine ingredient. Pray in love and it will be answered.

"Do everything in love."
– 1 Corinthians 16:14

Finally Paul closes his letter with the ultimate benediction. "Do everything in love" – enough said.

Grace is a Place

Lawville is a place where a lot of people live. In Lawville there is a lot of talk about a place called Grace but very few who actually find it.

The rulers of Lawville despise the notion of a place called Grace. They insist that Grace defies human reason. Still some in Lawville dream of living in Grace,

Residents of Lawville try to create and govern their own civilization by laws and commandments, which are good, but impossible to keep. All of the citizens of Lawville are lawbreakers. They like to think that they are not breaking the laws but in fact they flagrantly break the laws. Lawbreakers do not think the laws apply to them. But they do like to condemn others for breaking the laws and want to see others punished for their crimes.

Some in Lawville have heard of Grace and dream of one day escaping to live in Grace.

Residents of Grace live in love (agape). Grace people are welcoming and inclusive. Those seeking asylum to Grace are always granted immunity.

Inhabitants of Grace are not subjected to any background history or credit check. Grace does not have a police department or courthouse, because Grace does not have any laws. All the partakers of Grace have everything in common It is not communism because it is totally voluntary. People of Grace live in a state of innocence.
People of Grace live in freedom

Grateful are those who are covered by Grace's love.
Grace is a gift of God.

GALATIANS

The letter of Paul to the Church at Galatia admonishes believers who have returned to a legalistic observance of laws to achieve the approval of God. The practice of legalism is detrimental to grace. Grace is a place of innocence where our righteousness is in the **gift** of God.

> *"Are you so foolish? Having begun in the Spirit,*
> *are you now being made perfect by the flesh?"*
> – Galatians 3:3

Down through the ages religions of the world have established commandments, regulations and rituals as a means of being justified before God. While it is true that commandments and laws do provide a standard for righteousness, in reality they become an indictment of our failure to keep the righteousness requirements of God. Paul reminds the church at Galatia that "justification" is a gift of God achieved by faith in Jesus Christ.

The "law" points to a righteousness that is impossible to achieve through human effort. The invitation of God is to accept forgiveness and righteousness as a gift, by faith in Jesus Christ. As hard as it is to comprehend, this gift of grace cannot be bought, earned or paid back. Our human psyche refuses to believe that salvation is free and without a catch. This is why the Galatians feel that they must do something to stay compliant.

> *"Know that a man is not justified by observing the law, but by*
> *faith in Jesus Christ. So we, too, have put our faith in Christ*
> *Jesus that we may be justified by faith in Christ and not by*
> *observing the law, because by observing the law no one will be*
> *justified."* – Galatians 2:16

Recently I was totally convicted of my behavior and attitude toward those I cherish and love. I was not aware of it until someone brought it to my attention.

The problem is spiritual pride and self-righteousness. How easily we are deceived by our own illusions of grandeur. We glory in our own self-worth, our self-approval and our own self-righteousness as if we are accomplishing a great deal for God.

As we begin to take pride in our own efforts, our obedience, our self-denial (as if we attained it or accomplished it) we become conscious of our ego and believe we are just a little better than others. At this point we have fallen from grace!

> *"It is no longer I who live, but Christ lives in me; and the life which I now live in the flesh I live by faith in the Son of God, who loved me and gave Himself for me."*
> – Galatians 2:20

We cannot ever trust in our own goodness, our own accomplishments, our self-denial, our ability, our talents, our gifts, our knowledge, our self-worth, our education, our service or anything we posses or do for the Lord; for our standing is by GRACE ALONE!

How long will it be before we discover we cannot impress God with anything in and of ourselves? How long must we stumble and fall from grace and realize we cannot earn, or merit God's favor? We are sinners saved by grace! It is the gift of God and it can only be received through our Lord Jesus Christ. Our relationship is not based on performance but upon love and grace.

> *"I do not set aside the grace of God; for if righteousness comes through the law, then Christ died in vain."*
> – Galatians 2:21

A claim to salvation by human achievement would mean that the death of Jesus Christ was for no reason. Any attempt to add anything to the finished work of Christ on the cross would be an insult to his sacrifice, death and victory.

The truth is we are all here together and the same grace that was given to me is available to everyone and it is by the grace of God, I am what I am.

I have learned that when I drift from grace. I become conceited, self-righteous, arrogant and prideful. Slowly I begin to look down on those around me and slowly I fail to love them.

"You, my brothers, were called to be free. But do not use your freedom to indulge the sinful nature; rather, serve one another in love. The entire law is summed up in a single command: "Love your neighbor as yourself." – Galatians 5:13-14

The freedom that grace brings also provides a peace in our spirit. As we feel the heavy burden of condemnation, guilt and shame lifted from our shoulders we begin to feel a release of the Spirit of Love flowing into us and as we open our channels of compassion to others the love begins to flow through us and the Spirit begins to break forth into blossoms of gifts, flowers of charity and fruit of the Spirit.

> *"Life without love is like a tree without blossoms or fruit."*
> – Kahlil Gibran

"The fruit of the Spirit is love, joy, peace, forbearance, kindness, goodness, faithfulness, gentleness and self-control."
– Galatians 5:22-23

Galatians 5:22 is a profound and insightful picture of the mature Christian character. I recommend memorizing this verse and recognizing the fruit of the Spirit as a manifestation of a healthy happy life.

EPHESIANS

Paul writes to the church at Ephesus like he is the executor of a will. He explains to the believers in Ephesus that they are the benefactors of a spiritual trust, a blessing and inheritance that God intended since the beginning of creation. In love, God has adopted us as his children and made us holy (complete, perfect) and blameless (sin free) in Christ.

The genesis of God's plan was incepted in love.

"Praise be to the God and Father of our Lord Jesus Christ, who has blessed us in the heavenly realms with every spiritual blessing in Christ. For he chose us in him before the creation

of the world to be holy and blameless in his sight. In love he predestined us for adoption to sonship through Jesus Christ, in accordance with his pleasure and will - to the praise of his glorious grace, which he has freely given us in the One he loves."
– Ephesians 1:3-6

Paul further provides insight into the spiritual anatomy of the believer by defining their new nature in Christ. He describes the "new being" as a hybrid of the human being and the Christ Spirit. The Christian is a new creation with a deposit of the Christ Spirit, an immortal being filled with the power of love.

Paul exhorts and edifies this apostolic assembly to be rooted and established in **love** and to come to the full comprehension of **love** of Christ.

Paul's prayer for the followers of Christ is to be strengthened by the Spirit to be full of power and love, their new purpose and the essence of God.

"For this reason I kneel before the Father, from whom every family in heaven and on earth derives its name. I pray that out of his glorious riches he may strengthen you with power through his Spirit in your inner being, so that Christ may dwell in your hearts through faith. And I pray that you, being rooted and established in love, may have power, together with all the Lord's holy people, to grasp how wide and long and high and deep is the love of Christ, and to know this love that surpasses knowledge— that you may be filled to the measure of all the fullness of God."
– Ephesians 3:14-19

What Paul is praying for is what I have been trying to put into words in the chapters of this book. We were created in Love, by Love, for Love, to be Love.

"Speaking the truth in love,"
– Ephesians 4:15

A carnal and worldly person uses "speaking the truth in love" to hate and judge. They claim a pious self-righteous authority over and against people and their behaviors as a means of excluding unwanted people from their fellowship They criticize behaviors or customs they are unwilling to accept or people they do not wish to associate with. They use terms like "I may have to love them but I don't have to like them." These phrases are just walls to justify an unwillingness to extend grace, forgiveness, love and reconciliation. Judgment is always condemning and seeks a punitive action; where discernment exhorts, edifies and desires restoration. Paul expresses a respect for diversity and a call to unity when he expresses the truth in love.

> *"Hate the sin, love the sinner."*
> – Mahatma Gandhi

Mature Christians need to be careful not to judge anyone even those who violate the meaning of "speaking the truth in love," because in doing so we become guilty of violating our own teaching. Instead of judging, mentor discipleship in your relationship with immature Christians and provide love as the more excellent way and destination.

> *"Nothing can bring a real sense of security into the home except true love."*
> – Billy Graham

The truest test of Christianity is how I am treating my Mother and Father, my brother or sister, my children, and my neighbor. How loving I am and how kind I am, from day to day, to all men everywhere and anywhere. "Yes! "even the ones I do not know, the ones on the street corner, the ones that are not like me, the one who don't worship like me, or pray like me or go to church like me:

The ones who are sinners just like me!
I should love them, just as I love myself!

PHILIPPIANS

Paul enjoyed a special relationship with the Church at Philippi so he wrote them a personal expression of his love and affection. In his letter he writes of humility, self-sacrifice, unity, joy and Christian living. But overall he prays for the knowledge of love to increase, flourish and mature.

"This is my prayer: that your love may abound more and more in knowledge and depth of insight, so that you may be able to discern what is best and may be pure and blameless for the day of Christ, filled with the fruit of righteousness that comes through Jesus Christ—to the glory and praise of God."
– Philippians 1:9-11

Paul expresses to the church the joy he feels. Paul's desire is for his joy and their joy to increase. His formula for increasing joy is mental unity and covenant love. Communal harmony and individual wellbeing fosters a maturity and symbiosis of spirit and mind.

"Therefore if you have any encouragement from being united with Christ, if any comfort from his love, if any common sharing in the Spirit, if any tenderness and compassion, then make my joy complete by being like-minded, having the same love, being one in spirit and of one mind." – Philippians 2:1-2

Love is the motive for all that Paul writes. The letters of Paul are all love letters to the churches that he planted and nurtured. He expressly taught that faith and love were the hand and glove of the body of Christ. Through his devotion, discipline and doctrine he offered Spirit guided faith, hope and love as the primary principles to Christian living; …**but the greatest of these is love.**

GI Joseph

The airport atrium window brings cascades of sunshine into the heart of the terminal but on a rainy day the gloomy overcast sky and torrents of rain can convey misery and depression into the heart of any susceptible subject.

The USO is on the third floor and most of the soldiers lounge around with their computers and backpacks, trying to kill time, waiting for their flight back to the war zone. On the backside of R and R leave most of the troops are sad about leaving the comforts of home, friends, family and loved ones - returning to the God forsaken rocks, rubble, desert and dust of the theater.

Looking upward into the dreary atrium eye, out of my peripheral vision, I saw a speck of a person on the fourth floor balcony, a soldier, out of place. My spirit tingled and an inner voice screamed, help. I made a bee line to the elevator and slowly approached the isolated sergeant. His arm had stripes down to his elbow and I knew he was a high ranking NCO, a Chief Master Sergeant. As I approached he was grabbing the chrome rail like a vice grip with his white knuckles cinching.

"You look like you could use a friend." I said to him, as I cautiously approached.

"I don't want to lose it on the plane," he choked. "I am afraid I will let my troops down. I just want to kill myself here so I won't lose it in front of the other soldiers. "

"So what were you thinking about?" I probed. "Surly you weren't thinking about jumping off this balcony? You would probably only break a few bones, bust up your head and end up paralyzed. You don't want that. Do you?"

"Yea, you're probably right this isn't high enough," he quipped.

I dug deeper, "Why are you afraid of losing it."

"It's a long story," he said sadly.

I said, "Would you like to come into my office and tell me about it? I've got all day,"

He reached down and grabbed his hundred pound pack and nodded.

Once inside my office he sat in one of the chairs and put his head into the palms of his hands and wept a second.

He began to speak, "Chaplain, I am a career soldier. It's what I do. I've been in for 18 years. I re-upped two years ago and I have two years left until I can retire. This is my third trip back to Iraq. I've been there 12 years. But this last trip home my wife gave me divorce papers, my daughter is living with some guy and my son is running with some punks, in a gang. My wife tells me that she didn't get married so that she could live alone with no man in her bed. She said that she needed someone and I wasn't there. So she left me for another man. My daughter won't come home and my son won't listen."

"I have made a mess of everything."

"All of the reasons I have for being a soldier are gone!"

He was very stressed at this point. I affirmed his emotional pain, "That is a tough situation. I can see why you are so upset. You have sacrificed so much for your country and family and now you feel your reason for living is gone."

"Yea, everything I am fighting for no longer exists." he cried.

I looked him in the eye and said, "I am a military brat and a vet. I can understand a lot of what you are feeling. My dad fought in Vietnam and Korea and he was overseas for many years. My mom had to raise four kids. But once my dad retired, he was able to come home and makeup for all the years we missed. You can't change the past and you can't go AWOL. You are a loving man, a loving father, and a good provider. Your wife may have left you but there are hundreds of women who are looking for a man just like you. You are still a good man, with plenty to offer. Your children will still need you even though you may not see it now. Stay in touch with your children and pray for them. Give your situation to God and trust Him, love God and love your children and let them know how much you love them, and live your life with God in your heart. God loves you, I love you and your country loves you."

I could see strength returning to his countenance.

He picked up his chin and said, "I know that Christ is real and I know that Christ can get me through this. I have to renew my faith and recommit my life to Jesus Christ. I want to be the man God wants me to be. Would you pray for me, Chaplain? "

"Sure," I whispered. "Loving God, we try so hard to be good and do the right things in life but so many times we mess up and situations spiral out of control. Please forgive us for our failures, cleanse us through Christ, renew our spirit by your Spirit, and help us to love You and let You love through us.

Lord console Sergeant Garcia and use him for your glory. Send your Holy Spirit to be with his children, guard, guide and protect them until their father returns. Protect Sergeant Garcia, put a hedge of protection around him, lead him into your perfect will. In Jesus name I pray."

Sergeant Joseph Garcia was a different man when he rose to his feet. He thanked me and said he felt much better. I told him to check in with the military chaplain when he landed. He assured me he would.

Many soldiers suffer from PTSD, depression and abandonment issues related to their families. The protracted war is taking a toll on many of them. The Airport Chapel and our chaplains are the last point of human contact for these soldiers before they return to war. Our chaplains have prayed with literally thousands of soldiers and have helped literally thousands accept Christ and find inner peace.

Love is the Answer

> *"I love you, and I don't even know you. I choose to love you. You may not love me, but I love you because this is who I am."* – Chester Cook

I made a covenant with the God of Love that I would love unconditionally. Keeping this covenant is my daily vow. As I feel my reservoir being depleted I draw upon the Source of Love who always supplies all of my needs according to His riches in Glory.

During my quest for love, the closer I came to Love's Holy Grail the more resistance I encountered. I began to experience a tremendous amount of opposition from religious people. I was strangely attacked by many of my closest relationships. I even endured a series of assaults from people who were my associates in ministry. I began to feel like Joseph being thrown into a well by his brothers. The resistance only strengthened my resolve. My desire to become agape and practice perfect agape was challenged by many of my Christian brothers and sisters. I now know that the carnal nature is resistant to true agape, in the same way a child hates spinach. I also believe that the enemy of agape was trying to outflank the publishing of this book. Still I was determined to follow "the way" of agape.

If you think you are a loving person - think again. As committed as I am, I still recognize how much more I have to go to be perfect agape. I still have moments of weakness that cause me to fall. I still have a long way to go.

The daily practice of agape is far deeper than anything we can comprehend. It requires complete surrender and focus. It requires a singleness of purpose and a concentration on the person of Jesus Christ. The distractions of life do easily dissuade, deter and discourage the perpetual practice of perfect agape. The commitment to agape is continually undermined and crucified by self-interest, self-aggrandizement, and selfishness.

> *"What the world needs now is love, sweet love; No not just for some but for everyone."*
> – Burt Bacharach

We must be vigilant to keep focused on the commitment to agape at all cost.

It is true that Christians, in name only, have committed horrible crimes of violence in the name of God, using God's name in vain for their own personal agenda. All I can say is God forgive them and I am sorry for this callous misrepresentation of the Christian mission.

Atheist, people who choose to believe there is no God, may try to convince others that they can be moral people without a belief in a deity. And this may be true but it still remains true that the universe has this mysterious component of divine energy called love that causes people to do very powerful and valiant acts of heroism. Why?

It is also true that the existential concepts, "Law of the Jungle" and "Survival of the Fittest," are the mottos of those who choose to disavow any knowledge of God. In this kind of atheistic world view whoever has the biggest gun gets to be the king of the hill. Those who have no fear of God or the possibility of facing God and being held accountable for their actions argue; take, steal, kill; party like it's 1999; grab all the gusto that you can get; enjoy your life here on earth while you can; you only live once; this is all there is. Sadly for the atheist this futile fatalism is all there is.

> *"From dust we came to dust we shall return."*
> – Ecclesiastes 3:20

However, if you believe in God and you believe that life is mysteriously sustained and connected by the Spirit of Love, then it is imperative to be synchronized, in love and purpose, with the way, the truth and life.

There is a remnant of lovers who believe that agape will ultimately prevail over evil and that the Lord of Love will rule in the hearts of the subjects in the Kingdom of Love. One heart at a time the Spirit of Love is being birthed into the spirits of the believers. I choose agape. Will you accept the invitation?

Are you up to the challenge, to agape with every ounce of your being?

MAKE AGAPE YOUR VOW.

AGAPE.

APPENDIX 1

Lecia L. XXXXXXX

287 S. XXXXXXX Blvd.
Suite XXX
Beverly Hills, CA 90211
Phone (XXX) XXX-XXXX
Fax (XXX) XXX-XXXX

June 5,

Via Facsimile No. XXX-XXX-XXXX

Mrs. Xxxxx Xxxxx
Customer Service Manager
Hartsfield-Jackson Atlanta International Airport
P.O. BOX 20509
Atlanta, GA   30320

RE: Rev. Dr. Chester R. Cook and the Interfaith Chapel

Dear Mrs. Exxxx:

This letter is written to inform you of an amazing experience I had at your airport with Rev. Dr. Chester R. Cook, Senior Chaplain/ Executive Director of the Interfaith Chapel at the Hartsfield-Jackson Atlanta Airport.

On June 4, I found myself in the Delta terminal at approximately 6:00 a.m. in a state of crisis. I was supposed to return to Los Angeles on June 12, but was forced to leave early due to some very unfortunate events that transpired while I was visiting Atlanta.

When I attempted to book a flight at the Delta ticket counter, I was told that I would have to purchase a new ticket in the amount of $288.00 in order to return home. I was also told that my options were to 1) wait until June 12; 2) pay $288.00; 3) go to other airlines to compare prices; and, 4) contact Priceline to see if they would give me another ticket. None of the options presented were viable because I did not have enough money or resources to pay a fee or the price of a new ticket.

Concerned, but not without hope, I went to have a seat to think things out. I saw a sign that said Interfaith Chapel and decided to go to pray about my situation.

When I walked into the Chapel, I saw a sign that said there was a Chaplain. I also saw a sign that said the Interfaith Chapel provides certain emergency type services to those in need. I decided to wait for the Chaplain and see if he could assist me.

At approximately 8:30 a.m., in walked Rev. Dr. Chester R. Cook. We chatted about the events that led to my having to terminate my visit earlier than anticipated. He then offered to pray about the situation. After he prayed, he told me he would go to speak to Delta's highest ranking employee, yet he couldn't make any guarantees. He returned shortly thereafter and informed me that we had to wait for a telephone call to find out the results of his inquiry.

While we were waiting for the telephone call, Dr. Cook began to minister to me about the power of God and what it means to have total trust in God for our lives. He reminded me that absolute faith requires trust and acceptance of any means God chooses to work out solutions in our lives. We also spoke of the theology of love.

Forty five minutes into our conversation, the Delta representative phoned and stated that she had booked me on a flight leaving Atlanta at 4:00 p.m. but I would have to pay a $100 booking fee. Well, we still had a problem because I didn't have the $100. Dr. Cook suggested I call someone to pay by credit card and if they couldn't do it over the phone, they could pay into the Chapel's PayPal account and he would then pay the fee on my behalf. He also stated if that was not an option, then he would have to research other sources to raise the money.

When I went to the ticket counter, I asked what was the fee for the new ticket. The agent initially told me it was $50. He then read the notes further and told me I was good because there was no fee. All I needed to do was check my bags. He also told me that I had been given an excellent seat, which proved to be true. I was in the first row after first class with plenty of leg room and comfortable seats.

I immediately returned to the Chapel to tell Dr. Cook the good news. We were both astonished at how God had worked out the situation. Dr. Cook then ministered to me more about the power and love of God and what that means. Overall, it was an amazing experience that not only blessed me to be able to return home safely, but also blessed and uplifted my spirit.

You are to be commended on your selection and retention of Dr. Cook. I experienced a man of faith put love and action into deeds that resulted in a lesson of a lifetime and a testimony of which I can speak for years to come.

In reviewing your website, I note that it is your mission to be the world's best airport by exceeding customer expectations. I have had so many negative experiences at airports across the country since 9/11, however, thanks to Dr. Cook and the outstanding Delta representative, your mission was accomplished in that my expectations were clearly exceeded. Your airport is without question properly in the "best of class" category as is Rev. Dr. Chester Cook.

Sincerely,

Lecia L. XXXXXX

APPENDIX 2

David was my boss for many years before I entered the ministry. He did not have a lot of room in his life for God because of his career and bachelor lifestyle. I shared Jesus Christ with him several times but his spirit was unresponsive. After I became a minister I continued to pray for David. One day he called me on the phone and asked me to perform his wedding. I was shocked. Then he shared that he was a believer now. I was more shocked.

(I asked David to tell me his story – as told by David)

David and Brenda

Brenda and I met in 2000. What seemed like a casual meeting has turned into the most wonderful 9 years of my life.

Brenda was going through a divorce that was not easy. Her husband had been unfaithful several times and she found out about several of the encounters at about the same time. I had just ended a three year relationship with a woman that I thought was the one I wanted to marry. She revealed through her actions that she was not interested in marrying or at least not interested in marrying me. I decided to return to the life of being single. Marriage was for other people. I vowed to remain single.

During our first dinner date Brenda seemed different than any women I had dated. Engaging, warm, goodhearted, and honest were my first impressions. As I got to know her better other qualities became evident, her importance of family, her sharing with others and her belief in God were all part of her. She had raised two wonderful daughters practically by herself; she had to be well grounded.

Me, I was in my own world. I was single, I had a great job with money in my pocket and living on my houseboat. What a life! Why do I need to disrupt that life by getting married? That is what was controlling me.

In about March 2004 we had "THE TALK." The one that most men don't want to have and the one that most women (rightfully so) must have. Questions that Brenda needed answered were questions for which I had no answers. I ran to my cave, my houseboat. There, I could hide and not answer the questions until I had the answers.

I took several months to really reflect on my life. I even went to a counselor. Why was I afraid of marrying Brenda? I had grown to really respect and love her as a person. Her five brothers, her friends, her neighbors, her coworkers, everyone who knew her spoke volumes about her as a person. I even discussed it with my mother, one of the wisest persons I have ever known. She loved Brenda very much and thought of her as an "old soul", a real person. Mom saw the calmness in her that was evident through Brenda's deep belief in God.

By October of that year, I had worked out my own demons and decided that I did not want to live out my life alone and I did not want to lose Brenda. It was not easy making that decision, but I knew I would never find a more compatible mate.

How did I find the courage to give up my bachelor life? I am not sure, but I believe and thank God every day that He influenced my decision. I did not always rely so heavily on God's power to help me find my way. I have always been a believer and spiritual, but I kept it suppressed. Since I was desperate and unable to make a decision, I turned to God through prayer and asked him to help me make the best decision for Brenda and me. I did not want to marry her just because I was afraid of losing her. I knew this was selfish and would not have a happy ending. I wanted to marry her for all the right reasons and I needed to feel those reasons deep into my soul. Only God could help me with that and He did. We were married in May 2005 and every day I grow more in love

ith Brenda and stronger in my belief in God's love and power.
Brenda has taught me to put my faith in God and He will help me
carry my burdens and help me through the uncertainty of life. I
am so thankful that she has helped me establish building blocks
to strengthen my relationship with God and awaken the desire to
know Him more. We never know what direction our lives will take
or when we will need to turn to Him for strength and guidance.

In August of 2008, I fell from the attic through the ceiling and
landed on a ceramic tile floor. I shattered my left shoulder and left
foot. It could have been worse had I landed on my head! A year
later, I am still healing. Further surgery on my foot was needed
and probably another surgery on my shoulder will be required.

In November of 2008, my dear and wonderful mother passed
away. She had always been my rock. The one person I could turn
to for advice and inspiration. My father died when my brother and
I were young. Mom made many sacrifices to keep a roof over our
heads and food on the table. I learned so much from her.

In December of 2008, I lost my job of thirty plus years with
the same company. The economic downturn caught up with the
company and they had to make drastic cuts just to survive. Sixty
years old and having to start a new career is not an easy thing. A
year later and I am still without a job.

In March of 2009, Brenda was diagnosed with stage three
ovarian cancer. Chemotherapy and surgery has controlled the
cancer and she is cancer free today. The doctor called it a miracle
but we know that it was God's work. The doctor says there is a
50% chance it will return, but we continue to pray that it will not.
She has been so strong through all of this and continues to give me
strength through her positive attitude.

How quick our lives can change. Why have Brenda and I had
so much adversity in our short time together? Our lives were so
perfect! I cannot answer this question. I believe that God puts
on us only as much as we can handle and that he will test us. I
told Him this during prayer. I said "God, I know that you will test

us, but I believe I have passed the test. It is time to move on to someone else", perhaps a selfish prayer.

Brenda and I contend that we have been able to face these adversities through our own prayers and through the prayers of so many others.

As time moves on, my belief in God's power grows. I am becoming more comfortable with openly talking about His greatness and how it can change one's life. I credit my beloved Brenda for this. It all started because of her faith. She showed me the way. God sent her to me to complete my life. I know this to be true.